Türkiye as a Stabilizing Power in an Age of Turmoil

FAHRETTİN ALTUN

Türkiye as a Stabilizing Power in an Age of Turmoil

Library of Congress Cataloging-in-Publication Data
Names: Altun, Fahrettin (author)

Title: Türkiye as a stabilizing power in an age of turmoil | Altun, Fahrettin
Description: Washington : Academica Press, 2021. | Includes references.

Identifiers: LCCN 2021946303 |
ISBN 9781680537581 (hardcover) | 9781680537598 (e-book)

Türkiye as a Stabilizing Power in an Age of Turmoil

FAHRETTİN ALTUN

ACADEMICA PRESS
WASHINGTON~LONDON

CONTENTS

ABBREVIATIONS

AFAD, Disaster and Emergency Management Authority

AK Party, Justice and Development Party

BBC, British Broadcasting Corporation

COVID-19, Coronavirus disease 2019

DI, Development Initiative

EU, European Union

GDP, Gross Domestic Product

GNA, Government of National Accord (Libya)

HIV/AIDS, Human Imunodeficiency Viruses/Acquired Immunodeficiency Syndrome

IDPs, Internally Displaced Persons

ISAF, International Security Assistance Force

JMP, Joint Monitoring Programme (JMP) for Water Supply and Sanitation

KRG, Kurdistan Regional Government

NATO, North Atlantic Treaty Organization

NRF, NATO Response Force

OEF, Operation Enduring Freedom

OPCW, Chemical Weapons Convention

OSCE, Organization for Security and Co-operation in Europe

P5+1 Group, The UN Security Council's five permanent members (P5); namely China, France, Russia, the United Kingdom, and the United States plus Germany.

PKK, Kurdinstan Workers' Party, a terrorist organization. The PKK is listed as a terrorist organization internationally by numerous countries, including the members of the European Union and others such as United States, Canada, and Australia.

PPE, Personal Protective Equipment

PYD, Democratic Union Party. The PYD/YPG was set up under the control of the PKK terrorist organization in 2003.

R2P, Responsibility to Protect

SARS, Severe Acute Respiratory Syndrome

SETA, Foundation for Political, Economic and Social Research

UNSC, United Nations Security Council

TIKA, Turkish Cooperation and Coordination Agency

TRT, Turkish Radio and Television Corporation

UNHCR, United Nations High Commissioner for Refugees

UNICEF, United Nations Children's Fund

UNRWA, United Nations Relief and Works Agency for Palestine Refugees in the Near East

WHO, World Health Organization

YPG, People's Defense Units, set up under the control of the PKK terrorist organization in 2003.

PREFACE

Plato, the great classical philosopher, once said, "The measure of a man is what he does with power." As contemporary political leaders are faced with global challenges that threaten our world, how they use their power will determine humanity's collective future. Future generations will remember this moment distinctly and evaluate our endeavors and our failures based on what we could have done but did not. They will likely say that we could have come together around a common response in the face of a global pandemic, but we did not. They will be amazed how little effort we have spent in preserving the environment and slowing down climate change. They will hold us responsible for the plight of millions of displaced persons and refugees around the world. Yes, they will judge us and do it harshly because, honestly, we will have deserved it.

Still, it is not too late. The world's problems and challenges are monumental, and they require a global effort sustained over multiple generations. The ever increasing rate of interactions between human beings from many different backgrounds is creating a hyperconnected world. The speed of change is so extraordinary that it is simply impossible for one leader or one nation to keep up with and address the global challenges facing us. New problems and difficulties with global implications are born every second in different corners of the world. Within the last decade, the world faced critical challenges, including a major financial meltdown and global recession, the worst humanitarian crisis since World War II, the rising number of unending conflicts in different parts of the world, the emergence of new threats for international security, and the worst pandemic of our lifetime that cost the lives of millions and criplled economies across the world. The barrage of new challenges is unsettling societies around the world and today's leaders constantly find themselves in a difficult situation to address these problems. The fractured and dispersed nature of today's challenges is precisely the reason why humanity has no choice but to shape the future together.

This book is an effort to outline the overarching problems of the international system that is constantly failing humanity, especially the poorest and the most disadvantaged. It is a study not only to diagnose problems, but also to offer concrete solutions. The solutions presented here are clearly not exhaustive; however, they embody important principles such as the need to steer clear of exclusionary and nativist approaches. I intend to contribute to a constructive dialogue around the failures of the current system in the face of the most difficult challenges of our time. An honest conversation must acknowledge the fact that the failures of the international system undermine and destroy the lives of the least developed nations around the world. This is precisely why Türkiye under President Recep Tayyip Erdoğan has demonstrated its commitment to reforming the international system to make it more equitable and fairer for the world's most disadvantaged populations.

As the French scholar Michel Foucault once said, "I don't write a book so that it will be the final word." I obviously do not claim finality in any of my diagnoses or proposals. I provide my observations combined with my experience in government where I have witnessed firsthand some of the international community's biggest successes and simultaneously some of its worst failures. I hope that the result is a thoughtful exercise in meaningfully addressing the root causes of global paralysis, providing actionable solutions, and highlighting Türkiye's exemplary role.

My analyses and approach in this book will certainly be the subject of criticism, but I hope this criticism is constructive since that is the only way we can confront the global challenges of our time in a good faith effort and with our intellectual honesty intact. I hope that my attempt to provide a frank assessment of the global challenges facing our world will be received well and taken as a contribution to the debates on the future of the global system. If I can remind enough people of the perils of inaction, I will have accomplished the main goal of this endeavor.

President Erdoğan's lifelong struggle for our country has been the inspiration behind this book. His unique vision of Türkiye's development and his courageous leadership in the face of adversity continue to inspire us every day. His relentless pursuit of global justice and fairness must be an example for us all to follow.

I remain in deep gratitude to my family from whom I have been separated for long hours due both to my work and to the effort required to complete this study. I hope they accept this book as a token of my appreciation as I strive to contribute to a better future for our world.

INTRODUCTION

Today, the world continues to suffer from the shortcomings and failures of the international system. The COVID-19 pandemic demonstrated some of these failures including the lack of cooperation in the international arena to fix global challenges. In a short period of time, we have witnessed the absence of coordination across nations to tackle common problems, the ineffectiveness of international institutions to handle a global health crisis, and inequality in sharing the necessary equiptment and vaccinations, among others. These challenges have been present in the international system and generated humanitarian crises across the world. The COVID-19 pandemic made them more visible and more recognizable for the international public. In numerous instances, some wise policymakers and observers of global politics offered solutions to deal with them. One of the boldest proposals to fix the system and create a more equitable world order has been put forward by Turkish President Recep Tayyip Erdoğan.[1] This book is inspired by his vision and courage for a more sustainable and just future for our world.

More than three decades after the Cold War ended, the debate about a new international order, which essentially would revamp international institutions established during and following the end of World War II, has yet to reach a practical consensus. Existing institutions had already been proven insufficient to respond to the Cold War challenges. These institutions have often not been able to provide accountable, credible platforms for resolving regional conflicts, identifying and implementing a panacea for international crises in general, and organizing and distributing humanitarian aid to people affected the most in zones of international conflicts and hostilities. Nevertheless, despite such unresolved challenges in the international community, many remained optimistic about the future of an enlightened international system. Liberal internationalism was considered the invincible dynamic that would become the bastion of the new world order. In part, this optimism and the high expectations from a post-Cold War world caught the global community unprepared for the fresh challenges that began to unravel the existing world order.

In the 1990s, the world witnessed a more frequently occurring trend of civil wars, ethnic conflicts, and humanitarian disasters. This included the genocide in Rwanda, ethnic cleansing in Bosnia, and civil wars in different parts of the world. Contrary to expectations, there was no sign of waning of wars and international conflicts. Instead, there were an increasing number of bloody conflicts in different parts of the world. The humanitarian tragedies that occurred because of these conflicts could not be prevented by the international community. In addition, while many were expecting globalization to bring economic parity and equity to the developing world, the promises of fair distribution of its benefits went mostly unfulfilled. There was little sincere effort to assist developing nations in keeping pace with advances in business development and entrepreneurship as well as digital technologies fueling knowledge-based and service-focused industries. In addition to the north-south gap in the world, the new digital divide started to generate new forms of inequalities, such as inequality in accessing knowledge and information.

The international institutions formed in the 1940s were not suited to the far more rapid cycles of conflicts and hostilities around the world. The United Nations has failed, time and again, to respond in a timely manner to civil wars, exposing the inability of the UN Security Council to implement, much less enforce, its resolutions. In the absence of such enforcement, many belligerent actors took the opportunity to undermine the international order by destroying peace and stability. Moreover, the veto power of the Security Council's permanent members has become an impediment to achieving short-term solutions as a pathway to long-term sustainable peace and reconciliation in numerous disputes. In the words of Türkiye's President Erdoğan, the United Nations "has evolved into an institution that looks out for the interests of powerful nations instead of the entire world."[2] These institutions also failed to establish a framework and cooperation to fight poverty, underdevelopment, and economic inequalities.

In the first decade of the 21st century there was no time or breathing space for such issues, with the September 11 terrorist attacks in New York City and Washington, D.C. But, for the first time after World War II, countries around the world united in fighting against a common threat. The United States, for the first time in the history of the NATO alliance, for example, invoked Article 5, in assembling a diverse, multinational coalition to combat the global terrorist threat. Many countries around the world considered this period an opportunity to revitalize cooperation and coordination in national security policies and strengthen multilateralism. According to many, it could be possible to mobilize a truly global coalition that would bring together countries from all regions. At the end of the day, terrorism was a universally condemned phenomenon that had just proven its unprecedented global reach.

However, this optimism to confront global terror through a common strategy and shared solidarity proved to be short lived. Although countries around the world expressed solidarity and mobilized to provide support against terrorism, the main architect of the post-World War II international system, the United States, pursued a different path. Instead of revitalizing international institutions and strengthening corresponding initiatives, the U.S. set out to act unilaterally by dividing the world into "those who are with us or against us."[3] The 2003 invasion of Iraq by the United States and the behavior of U.S. foreign policymakers before, during, and in the immediate aftermath of the war, persuaded the international community that the world would never be the same again.

During Iraq's invasion, international institutions once again proved to be insufficient in stopping war or the fallout from it in its aftermath. The UN Security Council proved to be futile in stopping a war between UN member states. As terrorism became the primary focus of the major world powers' security establishments, nations paid less attention to finding points for global cooperation and adopted unilateral strategies and tactics. In addition to the difficulty of establishing a framework of cooperation in the fight against terrorism, the lack of a consensus about which groups to fight against generated significant challenges in this process. Several countries decided to be more selective in their fight against terrorism. While fighting against some terrorist organizations, their governments opted not to pursue specific organizations that they viewed as not being a terror threat to their nations. In the absence of a collective, globally organized, and clarified effort against the most serious common threats, global terrorism continues to be a specter, haunting nations, in every region of the world.

Two other crises solidified this emerging sense of unilateralism in the international realm. The SARS public health crisis of the 2000s was a major test for the international community in establishing a sustainable and functioning structure to deal with a public health crisis around the world, a point that would become painfully evident in early 2020. Today, every country has paid the price for missing an earlier wake-up call. Nations turned away from international cooperation, information sharing, and capacity building, and decided to deal with SARS with their own means. While questions remained about how the SARS virus originated, no mechanisms were enforced to make countries more transparent about such major public health risks. When the

COVID-19 crisis started in early 2020, neither individual countries nor international institutions were ready to handle such a major challenge. It was understood in a rather short period of time that the lessons of the SARS crisis were not studied properly by the international community. Despite the warnings by public health experts about the possibility of a new outbreak, the governments failed to prepare themselves for such a pandemic and international institutions failed to build capacity to handle it. Following the beginning of the outbreak, nations made the same mistakes as in previous epidemics and pandemics: they did not share information in a timely manner, they did not provide resources for international organizations to deal with the crisis, and they followed protectionist measures. All the superpowers in the international system contributed to this failure by adopting problematic policies.

The second crisis, which took place in 2008, brought the worst recession since the Great Depression. Just like the 1929 crisis, the 2008 Great Recession also originated in the U.S. However, in a short period of time, the crisis spread to other parts of the world and transformed into a global crisis. Nation-states were caught off guard. Many economies around the world faced rapid economic decline and high levels of unemployment. Once again international institutions proved to be inadequate in handling such a global crisis. The economic inequalities widened, making recovery that much more difficult for developing nations as the effects of the recession abated. In the aftermath of the crisis, the beginning of the great power rivalry between China and the U.S. contributed to the rise of protectionism and the emergence of trade wars. Instead of bringing complex interdependence, trade relations started to generate more tension in international relations. The subsequent COVID-19 recession in 2020 proved one more time that all nations are on their own in handling an economic crisis and there is no international cooperation framework for handling such crises.

The real aftershocks of these crises arrived in the second decade of the new millennium. The fault lines triggered after the U.S. invasion of Iraq dramatically impacted the Middle East, Civil wars erupted in multiple states in the region. Hundreds of thousands of people died in Syria and Yemen, while millions of people were displaced from their homes in both countries. These regimes violated international norms by committing war crimes and crimes against humanity. Terrorist groups emerged in conflict zones and threatened the security and stability of the region. Unlike expectations, the impact of these crises was not constrained within the countries of origin and started to be felt in different parts of the world, through the mass migration of people from these conflict areas to European countries, and the export of insecurity from failed states to different countries and regions via terrorist organizations. The civil wars have yet to exhaust themselves, given the diplomatic impasse as international channels and current conflict resolution mechanisms have failed to resolve the crises. Likewise, humanitarian disasters, such as in Yemen, have not been mitigated or resolved. Instead, international state actors have blamed one another for the emergence of an intractable "mess in the Middle East" rather than attempt to find points to cooperate in handling such crises.

Furthermore, major powers in the international system have played what can be described as destructive roles in the international system. While the U.S. has acted to significantly weaken existing international institutions, other major powers, such as Russia and China, have failed to provide solutions for the existing challenges within these institutions. Despite their rhetoric and their opposition to the unilateralism of the United States, they have failed to form effective multilateral institutions and international cooperation. The UN system, one more time, demonstrated its shortcomings during this period. The UN Security Council continues to be a ground for diplomatic gamesmanship and rivalry among major powers instead of finding consensus for achieving peace and global security. The calls for the reform of the UN system have fallen on deaf ears. The permanent members of the UN Security Council have become the biggest obstacle to establishing a more effective, representative, and functioning UN system.

Two other crises during the 2010s have raised questions about the viability of the existing world order. First, a crisis of sociological aftershocks followed the global economic meltdown that originated in the prior decade. Rising unemployment in Western countries and increasing disenchantment with globalization resulted in the rise of far-right and populist groups emphasizing nationalism. With the public blessings of opportunistic politicians, these groups added volatility to the historically centrist political discourse in Western countries. The rise of these groups led to political populism, xenophobia, and economic protectionism, targeting the globalization strategies and engagements of Western countries. Skepticism about global institutions and initiatives as well as criticism of international cooperation on issues including climate change, migration, and humanitarian disasters became more aggressive and divisive in tone. Populists objected to any form of global burden-sharing, including helping people in need during man-made and natural disasters. The "America-first" approach became a pattern that would be followed by other populists around the world. While they use the concept "America first," what they really mean has been "America only." Thus, any interaction with another country that could generate a win-win situation was considered unacceptable. To be part of international initiatives and to work within the framework of international organizations were regarded as acting against the national interest of the country.

One of the unifying characteristics of populists around the world has been their position against foreigners in their countries. The push against immigration, refugees, and asylum seekers has been strident, as far-right political parties and campaigns have capitalized solely on opposition to refugees. Islamophobia and anti-Semitism also rose rapidly during this period. There were some signs of rising Islamophobia in the aftermath of the 9/11 attacks against the U.S. Within the next few years, the rise of Islamophobia became a global phenomenon. In Western countries, a higher-pitched Islamophobia emerged in political discourse. Some politicians unashamedly endorsed the practice of profiling Muslims, banning the entry of Muslims into their countries, and curbing or limiting activities of Muslim organizations within their countries. Mosques and Islamic community centers have been targeted by extremist and neo-Nazi groups in Europe and the U.S. In Asian countries, there has been a similar sharp rise in anti-Muslim policies against the local Muslim minorities. Especially their religious freedoms have been significantly curtailed by governments. This wave of far-right extremism has also promulgated a foreign policy agenda of selective isolation. According to these groups, the international order was designed to be against the national interest of a particular country. Thus, any form of arrangement or commitment with other countries must be recognized as detrimental to the respective country's interests. Thus, these far-right movements have become a formidable force in dismantling the existing international order.

Finally, as mentioned above, the swift spread of the COVID-19 pandemic in early 2020 highlighted the existing unresolved challenges in the international order. Nations reacted quickly by closing their borders to international travel and following protectionist economic and trade policies. Major international institutions, including the World Health Organization, the United Nations, and NATO, could not muster collaborative efforts to deal with the pandemic. Even the most integrated and sophisticated regional integration entity, the European Union, failed to respond adequately in a timely manner as case numbers skyrocketed. In addition to shutting their borders, nation-states took a protectionist stance regarding medical devices (e.g., ventilators) and personal protection equipment (masks and protective garb for health-care workers). The competition for ventilators, masks, and even hand sanitizers aggravated tensions between nations and little was being done to aid countries which experienced some of the worst outbreaks in the early phase of the pandemic. For instance, in late February 2020, Italy and Spain ground to a halt as the death toll accelerated and hospitals were stretched beyond capacity. Yet even their closest partners in the EU failed to provide much needed assistance. The pandemic also exacerbated already deep rifts and inequalities among nations and among different social groups. The outbreak fueled rages of xenophobia around the world. As vaccinations have proceeded in 2021, access to vaccines parallels the issues witnessed in the previous year. The existing international order has demonstrated that it is ill-prepared in bringing a pandemic under control as was seen in the early stage of the COVID-19 pandemic and in the latter months of 2020. More importantly, the international community has lost its trust in numerous international institutions' ability and readiness to deal with such crises. Even as vaccinations are progressing and more countries are reopening their businesses, economies, and borders, there are still major concerns about how long the pandemic will continue before it is brought under full control. What became evident because of this crisis is that the world needs a better institutional framework to cope with crises of similar magnitude and impact such as climate change.

Against this backdrop of an unraveling of the international order, the increasing dysfunctionality of the international institutions, the deepening humanitarian disasters, and the rapid spread of civil wars and conflicts, Türkiye has called on the international community to act together to find solutions to the existing and emerging challenges. In all the aforementioned crises in the international system in the last two decades, the Turkish government suggested launching international initiatives to analyze and assess the problems and find solutions. On numerous occasions, President Erdoğan underlined the fact that it is not sustainable for the international system to pretend that the existing mechanisms, approaches, and institutions are sufficient in handling the system's current crises. Türkiye has sought to promote workable alternatives, particularly as it has seen its portfolio strengthen as a regional power in the Middle East. In the first part of the 21st century, the Turkish government has adopted a more proactive foreign policy in the region that is oriented toward mediating mutually acceptable solutions to long-term disputes. Türkiye has also offered suggestions about dealing on a broader scale with the issues of destabilization in the international order. There is a lot of room for revision and reformulation. Ankara has called for the international community to respond collectively to common global challenges while warning about the effects of falling into the trap of unilateralism. On climate, for instance, President Erdoğan has called on the international community to make it among our "top priorities at a time when conflicts, power struggles, and trade wars tend to steal the spotlight."[4] In many ways, when nations squabble over narrow self-interest and fight over restricting one another's influence, global threats like climate change and pandemics that can only be tackled through robust international response consume our planet. The existing institutions regularly fail to address these challenges at great peril to humanity and the environment.

From COVID-19 to millions of displaced refugees, there is no doubt that in order to address more effectively these contemporary crises a collective effort is essential in reforming international institutions. In its current autopilot mode, the international system will not bring about the stability to international relations that it once promised in the aftermath of World War II. Changes in governments and the election of more globally minded presidents and prime ministers to high office in Western countries alone will not bring long-term and meaningful changes to the international system. There are structural and ideational changes needed if the issues are to be addressed in the coming decades, especially humanitarian disasters caused either by war, famine, or climate change.

Türkiye's efforts in the last two decades have aimed to respond to these challenges, sometimes leading by example and sometimes by calling on the international community to reform certain structures, institutions, and mechanisms. Under President Erdoğan's leadership, Türkiye regularly encourages the international community to heed Türkiye's advice and follow the Turkish example in relevant critical matters while providing clear solutions. The latest example of this kind of leadership is President Erdoğan's concrete UN reform proposals outlined in his recently published book, where he declares, "The world is bigger than five" and argues for an enlarged Security Council membership structure that truly reflects the diversity and multipolarity of our world.[5]

The current book aims to provide a short synopsis of the last two decades through a narrative that explains how the unraveling of international institutions has occurred, and the failure of the international community to solve conflicts and international humanitarian crises. It will also focus on the emerging threats of populism and "country-first" approaches that challenge the essence of collegiality in a normally functioning global order. The book is divided into four chapters that address international institutions, humanitarian challenges, conflict resolutions, and the rise of far-right groups and "country-first" approaches. These chapters will present the current situation on the topic under consideration along with Türkiye's respective position on each topic.

Chapter Synopsis

The first chapter will focus on the historical origins of present failures, particularly on the delivery of humanitarian aid. During the Cold War, proxy wars turned developing countries into battlegrounds for the rivalry of U.S. and Soviet influence, while in the Middle East, Arab-Israeli wars led to an entrenched mode of tragedies. The international institutions established to handle such issues did not properly respond and when they did, they did not provide sufficient resources. After the collapse of the Soviet Union, the concern persisted. Due to civil wars and conflicts, within the last decade, the world has experienced a rapid increase in the numbers of refugees and internally displaced people. Amid this crisis, governments around the world have been reluctant to take steps to share this burden, refugee relief organizations have failed to meet the basic needs of people, and the international community has fallen short of bolstering the network infrastructure to deliver aid swiftly. In Syria, for example, as citizens fled attacks from their own government, the international community was slow to respond to the threat to human security. The Syrian problem serves as a microcosm of the broader issues related to humanitarian assistance to vulnerable populations.

In the same period, the inequalities among countries have also persisted. Despite successful poverty reduction campaigns around the world, during this period certain countries were left critically behind. Currently, around 730 million people around the world live in poverty, which is disproportionately distributed among regions. There are serious inequalities in terms of accessing public health and education in different parts of the world. So far, the humanitarian assistance that has been provided by the more developed countries has failed to suffice in resolving these major inequalities. Türkiye again tried to lead by example by increasing its humanitarian and development assistance to record levels. But, just like the refugee crisis, Turkish efforts alone cannot realistically resolve the holistic scope of disparities. Moving forward, the international system must address humanitarian disasters more decisively and in a timelier manner. Burden-sharing along with fair and equal distribution of humanitarian assistance to people around the world depending on their needs and the urgency of the situation should be an important underlying principle in prioritizing strategies and tactics. Meaningful steps are required to reverse mistakes and restore trust in the international system.

The second chapter will show how costly and consequential these institutions' failures have become to the global system. While there was a consensus in the international community that the international institutions should be more effective and functional in handling the existing and emerging challenges of the international system, there was not much willingness among the nation states to form new institutions or reform the existing ones. The UN and NATO do not only suffer from structural imbalances built into the international security system they support, but have also failed to address the plight of disadvantaged communities around the world. They have failed to address the emerging threats and risks in international security. This has been costly for the reputation and credibility of the international system which seems impotent in deterring bad actors from committing crimes against humanity, thereby aggravating already significant levels of regional instability and incidences of violating international norms.

The case studies presented in this chapter include the Cyprus issue, the Syrian conflict, post-war Iraq, the Iran nuclear issue, and Libya. In these foreign policy challenges, Türkiye has attempted to play a constructive role by pursuing a feasible overlap between its national interests and foreign policy objectives to serve regional stability and peace. The Turkish government always believes that a stable and peaceful environment allows Türkiye to safeguard its own national interests while elevating its regional role in a constructive way.

For example, Türkiye's aspiration to provide a resolution to the decades-old frozen conflict in Cyprus propelled Turkish conflict resolution efforts towards accepting the UN's Annan Plan, but the Greek Cypriot approach, emboldened by the EU, made a resolution impossible in the end. In its approach to post-war Iraq, Türkiye has always advocated for national unity, and an inclusive system of government that would not fall in the trap of sectarianism and would avoid the alienation and marginalization of ethnic and religious groups. Türkiye has warned against exclusionary policies toward Sunnis and of potential radicalization. Türkiye's mediation efforts on the Iranian nuclear issue have been aimed at lowering regional tensions and preventing a potential conflict between Iran and the international community. Türkiye sought common ground between the P5+1 group and Iran, judging that heightened tensions would adversely impact its national interests. During the Arab Spring, Türkiye sided with the people's grassroots power movements based on the idea that long-term stability and peace could only be achieved through the establishment of governments responsive to the demands of their people. Both in Libya and Syria, where the Arab Spring ended up creating civil war conditions, Türkiye sought diplomacy and political accommodation to prevent the countries' fracturing and disintegration. Later, before the U.S. withdrawal from the region, Türkiye also offered to host peace talks between the Taliban and the Afghan government. The Turkish government believed that to have sustainable peace in Afghanistan there should be dialogue among different groups and demonstrated its readiness to share the responsibility to facilitate such talks. In these examples, Türkiye not only sought its national interest but also the larger, long-term stability of the region. The case studies discussed in this chapter show that Türkiye has consistently pursued a conflict resolution approach by advocating in favor of a policy of regional stability and peace. Türkiye's efforts are significant but not sufficient by themselves to resolve these conflicts. The international community and other nations should share the burden, diplomatically, politically and economically, whenever it is necessary.

The third chapter focuses on unresolved conflicts that continue to destabilize regions and export insecurity around the world. This is another challenge where, over the last two decades, Türkiye has tried to lead by example in international relations. Long-simmering conflicts, many of which have been sustained in a frozen or dormant state by the absolute minimum of diplomatic effort, have extended in time and expanded in terms of geography. These conflicts have led to more bloodshed and violence in the respective regions and more disturbing incidences of war crimes and crimes against humanity. In the last two decades, Türkiye has engaged relevant actors on the ground while advocating for diplomacy and reconciliation in the international arena. As a stabilizing and stability-seeking power, Türkiye leverages the features of its democratic system, open market, economic resources, and security partnerships to contribute to regional conflict resolution efforts.

The power imbalance pervading the United Nations system is briefly discussed before proceeding to analyze the most concrete examples of this institution's failure to find solutions - namely the cases of the Israeli-Palestinian conflict, the Syrian civil war, and the COVID-19 pandemic. In the Israeli-Palestinian conflict, the multiple instances of a UN Security Council member's abuse of its veto power are discussed to demonstrate the fact that specific national interests of UNSC members have been systematically prioritized over the interests of the less powerful party in the conflict. In the discussion about the Syrian civil war, the chapter makes it clear that other members of the UNSC played similar destructive roles during the conflict and contributed greatly to the failure of the UN in stopping this war. The Assad regime's systematic violations of human rights could not be brought to the international community's attention in a meaningful way, given the aegis provided by some members. Negotiations among UN Security Council members seemed more intent on preserving the status quo of their corresponding regional strategic interests - be they economic and/or security issues. With the COVID-19 pandemic, the UN and the World Health Organization (WHO) faltered especially in their awkward initial response to the outbreak. The controversies arose about the organization due to its earlier response to the COVID-19 pandemic.

In the case of NATO, a similar pattern emerges in the way that the big powers' priorities take over and define institutional direction. Failing to mature and evolve within the new international system after the end of the Cold War, NATO has struggled to address the matters of refugee crisis, international terrorism, and pandemic response. The chapter discusses specific examples of NATO's failures to create a broad strategy for the post-World War II era, its inability to cope with the refugee crises emerging on multiple fronts, and how the lack of action has affected NATO allies in unproductive ways. This has extended to a lack of a coordinated response by NATO in defining how terrorism should be dealt with, embedding deeper a dysfunctional diplomatic culture that has proved unfortunate in confronting the spread of the COVID-19 pandemic. The chapter's conclusion makes plain the case for institutional reform and rehabilitation. Türkiye's position encompasses the simple broad statement that "The world is bigger than five," suggesting that a greater number of more diverse nations must be brought to the table. The international institutions, particularly the UN system, shouldn't be held hostage to the power rivalry between the international system's major powers. The organization's dysfunctionality and its lack of effectiveness against the current challenges are mostly due to the competition and rivalry among these major powers. Under these circumstances, it is impossible for the UN system to contribute effectively to the resolution of the most pressing problems in the international system.

The final chapter focuses on the rise of political populism, far-right extremism, and "nation first" approaches in the international system. In the last decade, the world has witnessed a sudden rise of far-right movements in all regions, affecting democratically elected governments. Opportunistic politicians have taken advantage of this wave by capitalizing on the shameless use of discriminatory and xenophobic language. This also has emboldened advocates of an isolationist foreign policy, which, in turn, has consolidated nationalistic anti-refugee positions in dealing with humanitarian crises and rigorous protectionist sentiments affecting global and regional trade. Islamophobia has also been heightened and Islamophobic discourse started to become part of the mainstream political rhetoric in many Western countries. Some governments have taken steps that violate basic religious liberties and the freedom of their Muslim citizens. Although Islamophobia is mostly regarded as a domestic political issue, the extreme exclusionary sentiments have spread to foreign policy discourses. More significantly, Islamophobia has become a global threat for the peace and harmony of societies across the globe.

In the last decade, Türkiye has warned the international community and especially Western nations about the dangers of far-right movements, with the added concern about its own diaspora in Western and European countries. For Türkiye, the rise of Islamophobia is very similar to the rise of anti-Semitism in Western European countries before World War II as it can generate the same threat to the lives of Muslims and other minorities. Ankara has also asserted that the discriminatory practices against Muslims, if not prevented, could lead to the rise of other forms of discriminatory practices, including anti-Semitism and racism. The issue has expanded beyond its earlier boundaries as far-right movements and governments have taken a harsh stance against refugees coming from the Middle East. In several elections in European countries, the parties with anti-refugee platforms have won sufficient pluralities or even outright majorities. Eventually, the targets of Islamophobia expanded to include all Muslims, regardless of their residency status. Türkiye has responded to the rise of Islamophobia by using different strategies. The Turkish government has facilitated international discussions about combating Islamophobia. President Erdoğan has brought these issues to the agenda of most international meetings and has called on his counterparts to take the necessary steps to prevent the spread of this ideology across the world Türkiye's strategy is intended to subvert the widely deployed discourse of "clash of civilizations" in geopolitics and international relations. As a co-chair of the Alliance of Civilizations Initiative, Türkiye has fought against Islamophobic and anti-refugee movements around the world in the hope of bridging confessional differences. Türkiye believes that if no action is taken, the damage to the existing international order might be so severe that it will be impossible to repair.

CHAPTER ONE

THE FAILURE OF THE INTERNATIONAL COMMUNITY IN HUMANITARIAN ASSISTANCE

The capacity to deal with human suffering can reinforce the confidence and trust nations place in the international system. The principal architects of the liberal world order following the end of World War II aimed to prevent wars and provide hope to people in need. They claimed to establish a world order that would facilitate these objectives. Institutions were established to ease the suffering of people and international conventions of laws were signed to protect human dignity. The architects of these institutions had hoped that two world wars within a span of less than three decades should not become a cycle, given the widespread destruction of property, the massive casualties, and the millions of displaced people, many of whom had to endure lifelong physical and psychological traumas. "Never again" became an aspirational mantra in the efforts to preclude the outbreak of another global war and massive human suffering.

The optimism in the post-World War II days turned out to be short lived, as new conflicts erupted and hostilities emerged anew in areas already scarred by war. The emergence of a Cold War between the Soviet Union and the United States significantly hurt the emerging optimism of preventing another major conflict in the international system. The intensification of ideological rivalry and the rising arms race between two superpowers changed the atmosphere of the entire world. To top it all, the two Cold War superpowers launched proxy wars in developing states. People there suffered from the intense fighting between the two ideological groups. Large sections of societies in these countries became refugees while the conflicts destabilized neighboring countries and, in some instances, the whole region. Civil wars along ideological lines spread like wildfire. In the Middle East, the Arab-Israeli wars generated a humanitarian tragedy that has yet to be acknowledged universally. The lands of Palestinians were occupied by the Israeli state, precluding Palestinians from living with dignity and forcing them to flee to neighboring countries. Millions have had to spend their lives in refugee camps while the Israeli state has built illegal settlements on their lands. In short, every war inadvertently causes displaced people, refugees, and tragedies that are manifested in painful memories and traumas decades after the hot war has ended. Meanwhile, international organizations and NGOs established to assist displaced citizens and refugees fell short of their founding principles, while committed aid workers could not receive sufficient resources and endorsements from the respective governments in affected areas to provide humanitarian services. When the war in Afghanistan created, one of the world's gravest humanitarian disasters, international observers in media and political and diplomatic circles were more attentive to the military outcome of the Soviet-Afghan war than to immediately responding to the dire conditions in the refugee camps. The war created a major destabilizing impact on the neighboring countries and exported insecurity in the region. However, the international community was, once again, not willing to pay attention and spare serious efforts to handle these challenges.

The end of the Cold War did not reshape this dynamic. In the early 1990s, the optimism and hope in yet another triumph of the liberal international world order proved to be as short lived as in the 1940s. Many had projected a world without major wars and without human suffering. There were even those who claimed that the end of the Cold War was the "end of history." The stable moment broke quickly with civil wars popping up all over, emphasizing how earlier optimism was mere wishful thinking. There was no preparation at the state, regional, or international levels on how to resolve a fresh wave of humanitarian crises, including large numbers of refugees - the most since the end of World War II. The international community acted as if paralyzed when it encountered the worst humanitarian crisis in Europe since World War II. The Bosnian War was a prime example. In the midst of Europe and at the height of dreams of a liberal world order, a humanitarian tragedy took place in Bosnia, an ethnic cleansing followed by a massive refugee flow across the continent. Subsequent conflicts in the 1990s affecting Somalia, Rwanda, and in Eastern and Southern Europe were also met by the international community's inaction. The world essentially shied away from efforts to ease the humanitarian suffering exacerbated by civil wars.

Moving into the 21st century, the international community did not seem to absorb the lessons from the humanitarian disasters in the decade after the end of the Cold War. Instead of establishing mechanisms and strengthening institutions for promoting the protection of vulnerable and oppressed groups, the international community relied on ad hoc solutions with the expectation that these crises would eventually disappear. The growing numbers of refugees, their living conditions, their lives and status did not constitute a priority for the international community. Xenophobia and Islamophobia in Western countries, which targeted the most vulnerable groups, namely refugees and asylum seekers from Asia and the Middle East, aggravated the refugee dilemma. States sought not only to lower the quotas of refugees from Muslim countries, but went to the extreme of trying to implement an outright ban by contending that migration constituted a national security threat. Ethnic and religious profiling of Muslims made it more difficult for them to travel abroad or seek sanctuary from civil wars, proxy conflicts, and persecution by autocratic regimes. In the first decade of the new millennium, the invasions of Iraq and Afghanistan produced humanitarian crises on a scale that became difficult to manage logistically, as the numbers of internally displaced people in these conflicts reached levels not seen since World War II. The Watson Institute estimated that by 2020, 9.2 million Iraqis were internally displaced or became refugees abroad. In the case of Afghanistan, affected by more than 40 years of conflicts and invasions first by the former Soviet Union and then the U.S., there are "currently more than 2.6 million registered refugees in the world from Afghanistan – more than one in ten of all refugees, and the second highest number after Syria."[6] The U.S. withdrawal from Afghanistan and the capture of its territories by the Taliban forces generated a new wave of refugees in the summer of 2021. Humanitarian organizations are expecting to see up to six million new Afghan refugees in this new period.

In other parts of the world, conflicts generated waves of refugees and displaced people. According to figures provided by the United Nations High Commissioner for Refugees (UNHCR), in the Darfur conflict, Chad is already hosting more than 3600,000 refugees and in early 2021, another 100,000 were displaced, a difficult development given the ongoing pandemic. These massive waves of refugees put the host countries in an extremely difficult situation. None of the host countries were ready to host this massive influx of people from mostly adjacent countries and none received sufficient support from the international community to handle these humanitarian crises. At one point, host countries assumed that refugees would be temporary guests, that the conflicts from where they fled would end shortly, and they could decide either to return and repatriate. But, as in Afghanistan, the conflicts became protracted. Refugees in host countries became ever more stressed and tense, and these feelings were transmitted to the domestic population that demanded their governments adress the plight immediately. As conflicts became protracted, in addition to food and shelter, refugees required comprehensive healthcare facilities, education for their children, and job training options. Rare was the instance in which an international organization could meet such needs in a timely manner. Meanwhile, the numbers of refugees continued to proliferate, meaning that existing resources were overstretched and refueling an already problematic cycle.

In June 2021, the Office of the United Nations High Commissioner for Refugees reported that there are 82.1 million "forcibly displaced people" around the world, representing more than one percent of the world's total population. The figure is likely higher given that the reported UN figures only account for people registered under the mandate of the UNHCR and the United Nations Relief and Works Agency for Palestine Refugees in the Near East (UNRWA). The UN numbers break down into 48 million internally displaced people, 26.4 million refugees, 4.1 million asylum seekers, and 3.9 million Venezuelans displaced abroad. More than two-thirds of refugees come from just five countries with Myanmar (11 million) and Syria (6.7 million) comprising the largest portion. At the end of 2020, Türkiye housed the largest number of refugees, with nearly 3.7 million people. Colombia is second with 1.7 million, including Venezuelans displaced abroad. The situation of forcibly displaced people is dire, particularly as there are 35 million children (under 18 years of age) who are at risk of hunger and starvation. According to the UNHCR, 80 percent of the displaced people under the UNHCR mandate are in countries and territories affected by acute food insecurity and malnutrition.[7] They also lack medical care, and, in some instances, refugee camps have become the epicenter of not just the pandemic but also of other illnesses and diseases. There were concerning reports and studies conducted by non-governmental organizations focusing on the state of COVID-19 pandemic in the refugee camps. For instance, the International Rescue Committee reported that the refugees in camps in Syria, Greece, and Bangladesh faced a heightened risk of spread of COVID-19.[8] In addition to its outcomes regarding the health of refugees, the outbreak also generated significant economic challenges for the administration of the refugee camps. In a report, Oxfam stated, "The pandemic also fueled hunger. Only half of the refugee households today have acceptable levels of food. Both refugee and host communities reported overwhelming difficulty to find sufficient or good quality food."[9]

The UNHCR also tracks the destinations of displaced people. Some 73 percent of the refugees are hosted by neighboring countries. There is a pattern in these humanitarian crises where people do not have other choices but to seek shelter in one of the neighboring countries closest to the conflict zone - a pattern that has been difficult to break given the encompassing sensitive security and logistical challenges. In the meantime, refugees with educational and career training already in their portfolios and means to relocate have sought out other destinations to rebuild their lives economically. Some did not shy away from trying to relocate farther away from their homeland. But the majority have stayed at their first destination, hoping to return to their homes within a relatively short time. More often, however, people in war-torn countries have had no other choice but to stay in their homes. The host country's willingness to extend the stay of individuals has burdened the economy along with adding political stress and testing the patience of public opinion. There are always politicians on the far right attempting to exploit the grievances of the host communities and inflame the tensions between refugees and citizens. They frame the refugees as scapegoats for the host country's problems, putting the governing political party on the defensive, which can distract officials from attending to the crisis behind such political tensions. Furthermore, many host countries may not be well prepared to host large numbers of refugees in their countries, as the UNHCR figures indicate that 86 percent of the refugees are hosted in developing countries and the least developed countries house 27 percent of asylum seekers.

Refugee relief organizations struggle to honor their mission by providing food, shelter, and health care. International organizations have set up camps, for example, that without question address the immediate concerns of the individuals and their families, but those same camps also often fall short of the standards the humanitarian community considers as norms for adequate care and access to essential needs. Likewise, host countries, which already have strained economic resources, are faced with difficult options, especially if they are concerned about violence impeding relief assistance, domestic political resistance, and the potential of destabilizing effects rippling across their country and spreading to the region. The rapid increase in the number of refugees in the host countries has not only strained the resources of these nations, but has also generated stress on the country's existing infrastructure. In Türkiye, for instance, in a rather short period of time, the population of Kilis, a town near the Syrian border, expanded dramatically as the number of Syrian refugees easily exceeded the town's original total population. Likewise, countries and communities are ill-equipped to prepare for a sudden, unexpected surge of refugees as opposed to a gradual flow of displaced families seeking refuge. Many towns do not have the economic wherewithal to sustain major sudden shocks to their economy, which can trigger significant jumps in real estate and food prices. Likewise, confronting a different sociocultural group generates tensions that cannot be readily resolved by edicts and mandates. Aid and support for the refugees, which comes from hasty and inadequate planning, can cause anger and envy in the lower economic classes of host communities. Law enforcement and security officials face the challenge of regularizing the refugee flow so as not to cause disturbances or violent responses in the communities. In some instances, even registering refugees can constitute a major challenge for the local governments. These concerns require more material resources to ensure the core public service infrastructure continues to operate even as the population they serve, in some instances, has doubled or tripled. The difficulty of communicating with the newcomers and cultural differences require active government intervention to ensure accommodation occurs with mitigated effects of tension and anxiety. Even as obvious as these concerns might seem, many entities have failed to coordinate efforts to ensure a smoother integration of refugees into the host communities, more frequently leaving the host countries to their own devices.

As noted earlier, the large representation of children in the refugee numbers also requires other forms of accommodation, especially in providing education and ensuring literacy is preserved and developed. Finding teachers, establishing temporary institutions, and preparing curricula have been among the most significant challenges, along with sensitized counseling services to help children deal with the trauma and stress arising from the forced displacement. Failing to provide critical educational services also aggravates risks of social and security problems for the host countries. At the same time, failing to provide education will widen the existing gap of inequality in host countries, which are already contending with the tensions of a substantial segment of marginalized youth in their communities. In addition, the absence of education makes youth vulnerable to radicalization as an outlet to express their frustration. In some instances, they become easy prey for criminal and terrorist groups around the world - potentially perpetuating a lost generation of youth, especially with the large numbers of children in the refugee population. Thus, hosting refugees requires not only hospitality predicated on community morals and ethics, but also a strategic international endeavor to provide assistance so that the prevailing risks of terrorism, security, economic disruption, and destabilized political environments are brought under control and mitigated.

The wave of Syrian refugees to neighboring countries following the beginning of the civil war is emblematic of these concerns. As the Arab Spring unfolded, the people of Syria launched demonstrations to hold the government accountable for the corruption in the country and mistreatment of civilians. Instead of listening to the Syrian people and taking steps to change the status quo, the regime in Damascus swiftly cracked down on the opposition, using live ammunition against the demonstrators to deter others from joining. The strategy led to a bloodbath in the cities of Syria and angered people who returned to streets. The regime's refusal to listen to the demands of the people and the growing number of casualties united large, diverse segments of the Syrian population. As a result, the demonstrations spread across the country. Seeing the increasing degree of the people's frustration and their insistence on demanding their rights, the regime deployed its air forces to bomb cities. Using indiscriminate violence against civilians, the regime aimed to kill not only those who joined the demonstrations but also those who might have participated. The number of casualties skyrocketed and the opposition to the regime increased substantially as well. Then, the regime turned to a new, more violent strategy, which caused a massive number of people to flee their homes for safety. Realizing that he could not silence the opposition using excessive force, Bashar Assad went further by depopulating cities through intensive fire power and threat of massacre. Once again, barrel bombs were used against civilians by the regime, while initial targets of these attacks included hospitals and bakeries. To force people to flee from their cities, regime forces seized the cities and prevented the flow of humanitarian aid and food stocks to the people in need.

During the movement of hundreds of thousands of civilians towards northern Syria, humanitarian workers and neighboring countries in the region worried about an uncontrolled humanitarian disaster. Yet, despite the urgency, the international community was slow to act on this emerging threat. While some international aid workers tried to reach the affected populations, the arrival of terrorist groups and their networks in Syria complicated the situation. Terrorist groups targeted opposition forces and exploited people fleeing their homes, both financially and physically. Finding themselves in a brutal government crackdown and on the receiving end of attacks and abuse from terrorist groups, Syrian civilians fled not only from their homes but also from their country. Neighboring countries were the first target of this massive exodus. The presence of highly populated city centers across northern Syria made Türkiye the most convenient and realistic destination for Syrian refugees. Syrians found it easy to pass to Türkiye and seek shelter from potential attacks by their own government.

The initial wave of refugees in Türkiye started soon after the beginning of the civil war in Syria. Immediately preceding their arrival, Turkish aid groups and affiliated agencies set up refugee camps and provided immediate shelter and food for these refugees. After seeing the Iraqi Kurdish experience during the Gulf War in 1991, humanitarian agencies in Türkiye were more prepared to handle such a flow from Syria. Following the liberation of Kuwait by the international coalition after the Gulf War, the Kurds rose up against Saddam Hussein alongside Shia forces. Saddam launched a massive offensive against these groups, which was not surprising given that he had previously ordered massacres of the Kurdish population, including the use of chemical weapons. Knowing that he had no qualms about using force against civilians, the Kurdish groups and Turkomans living in northern Iraq fled to Türkiye for their safety. In a short period, hundreds of thousands of refugees entered Türkiye from its southern border. Türkiye hosted these refugees until the establishment of a no-fly zone in northern Iraq, and eventually they voluntarily returned to their homeland. During this crisis, the Turkish government provided aid for the Kurdish and Turkoman refugees without the help of the international community.

When Syrians started to arrive in the early days of the Syrian uprising, Syrian refugees were hoping that it would be a temporary stay. Just like in the crisis in Iraq, the Turkish government followed an "open door" policy for those who fled from persecution. But the events in Syria turned into a protracted civil war following increasing use of military power by Bashar Assad against Syrian civilians. In Ankara, the Turkish government proposed that international organizations establish a no-fly zone in northern Syria to assure displaced people were protected against Syrian air forces and their bombing of the Syrian cities and civilians. In some towns and cities across the Turkish-Syrian border, a no-fly zone would allow civilians to remain safe either in their homes or within the borders of their own country. This would also impede the depopulating strategies of the Syrian regime through the use of force. In multiple bilateral and multilateral settings, Türkiye urged the international community to launch such an operation to save lives and deter the regime from committing crimes against the Syrian people. But this proposal was not welcomed by the international community and was summarily dismissed. Türkiye was aware of the humanitarian consequences of inaction in such a crisis; however, many in the international community rejected these warnings and took no actions to prevent such a humanitarian tragedy.

The crisis in Syria demonstrated that there were multiple opportunities for the international community to prevent the humanitarian disaster. The lack of a collective and determined action by the entire world against the Assad regime led him to escalate the degree of violence he used against his citizens. In the absence of any deterrent, he ordered massacres in front of the eyes of billions of people who were horrified at videos and images transmitted across social media platforms. Furthermore, when the international community failed to respond to the atrocities, the Assad regime considered this as a green light to continue its strategy of forcing people to leave their lands and move towards the borders with neighboring countries. The safe zone proposal was yet another idea to contain the crisis within Syria and prevent refugees from becoming sitting ducks for all kinds of smuggling networks. However, just like the no-fly zone idea that Türkiye offered, the safe zone proposal was also flatly rejected by the major stakeholders and major powers in the world. For the Assad regime, each point of inaction by the international community was another green light for taking more violent action against its own citizens. After the failure to set up a no-fly zone or a safe zone, Assad escalated the violence and indiscriminate destruction of cities and their infrastructure. As a result, the Syrian people sought sanctuary in other countries to save their lives. Neighboring countries such as Jordan, Lebanon, and Türkiye faced a massive flow of refugees. With the expansion of the conflict, these numbers continued to rise. Especially during Assad's bloody attacks on the opposition strongholds in northern Syria, every attack on a city generated a new wave of refugees heading towards the Turkish border. The use of chemical weapons by the regime and the emergence of DAESH in the region exacerbated the refugee crisis in the country. Those seeking refuge from the regime's atrocities, trying to save their lives from the violence of terrorist groups, and fleeing from horrible human rights abuses converged in Türkiye during the conflict.

During this period, Türkiye acted on its own following the failure of the international community to address the humanitarian disaster. In a move not widely acknowledged by the international community or by the media outside of Türkiye, the government in Ankara followed a humanitarian refugee policy towards Syrian refugees. As refugees poured in, Turkish aid agencies went through a steep learning curve to develop the infrastructure to deal with the burgeoning crisis. Syrians belonging to diverse ethnic and religious groups found safe refuge in Türkiye, and dozens of refugee camps were established to meet the needs of the refugee populations. Medical care was provided for free and with the support of some international organizations, refugees began receiving monthly allowances to buy food and other necessities. But, the rapidly expanding number of refugees stressed the logistics of humanitarian services, particularly in communities along the southern border of Türkiye, which hampered efforts to integrate refugees at least temporarily into the community.

Syrian refugees arrived in Türkiye during this time in astounding numbers. For instance, the city of Kilis, bordering Syria, had a population of 80,000 before the Syrian civil war. In less than five years, the city's population more than tripled to 250,000. In some instances, the flow of refugees spiked in such a short period that despite all preparations, it constituted a significant challenge for the Turkish government and civil society. During the crisis in Ayn al-Arab, for example, 180,000 mostly Kurdish refugees who fled from DAESH entered Türkiye in less than 48 hours. Such a massive flow of refugees within just two days strained the efforts of Türkiye's aid agencies. A similar massive flow of refugees occurred when the terrorist organization People's Protection Units (YPG) acted on its own in depopulating territories under the control of Sunni Arab and Turkoman groups in order to gain control of the territories in northern Syria. During the 2014 attacks by the YPG forces on Tal Abyad, tens of thousands of Turkoman and Sunni refugees entered Türkiye from Syria in a short period. Confounding efforts to control the refugee flow, Türkiye recognized that refugees were coming from areas representing nearly one-third of Iraq that had fallen to DAESH control. The Yazidis, a minority group persecuted during the Saddam Hussein regime and threatened by DAESH from Sinjar, fled to Türkiye. Soon after, members of every persecuted group in the Syrian and Iraqi civil wars came to Türkiye. Both the Assad regime and emerging terrorist organizations in Syria and Iraq were committing war crimes and crimes against humanity. Massacres and numerous incidents of indiscriminate killings could not generate the international reaction to compel states to launch an intervention in Syria and ensure safe cover for those who might have decided to stay.

This refugee flow also made Türkiye a target for terrorist organizations that committed crimes against the Syrians and Iraqis. They tried to export the conflict within the borders of Türkiye. The YPG is the

Syrian branch of the PKK, which Türkiye, the EU, and the U.S. consider a terrorist organization. The PKK has organized terrorist attacks against Türkiye for more than three decades. While the international coalition prioritized arming and equipping the Syrian offshoot of the PKK instead of the people in need and the moderate opposition entities in Syria, the PKK increased its attacks in Türkiye. It organized the deadliest terrorist attacks in the history of the Turkish Republic, targeting the most significant transportation hubs and city squares in the country. In addition, DAESH also organized several deadly terrorist attacks against the Turkish people. In addition to city centers, these two terrorist organizations also targeted towns and cities on the border. DAESH launched rocket attacks against civilians in Kilis, killing residents and targeting any form of gatherings, from rallies to weddings, to destabilize the region as a whole. Meanwhile, the PKK organized terror attacks targeting border guards and Türkiye's law enforcement units.

The rise of these terrorist groups during the civil wars securitized the refugee issue in Europe. This marked a critical turning point in the Syrian humanitarian crisis. The rise of DAESH and its attacks across Europe reached priority level for many countries. European nations started to see refugees as a security problem, and continued to be insensitive and to disregard the plight of Syrian refugees. Many Europeans started to perceive refugees as risks to their countries' national security. Some groups even accused refugees of the terrorist attacks in their countries. This attitude not only fueled anti-refugee sentiment among people in Europe, but also generated an atmosphere of fear among newly arriving refugees in those countries. On the other hand, Türkiye avoided securitizing the refugee issue and the government of Türkiye resisted endorsing or fueling populist anti-refugee discourse. The Turkish government spent a considerable amount of effort to educate the Turkish public about the crisis in Syria and to explain the plight of the people running away from their countries. Meanwhile, European countries sought precautions to control refugee flows into their countries. There was little effort on the continent to educate the public about the plight of refugees, and most European governments allowed the anti-refugee groups and their discourse to dominate the public space. Syrian refugees came to be regarded as usual suspects who constituted major threats to the security of their host countries. With more frequent attacks in the name of DAESH, although most were committed by homegrown terrorists, refugees were soon framed as scapegoats for disrupting the stability of the affected communities. The irony is that most terrorist attacks in these years did not occur in these European countries but in Türkiye against Turkish citizens. Despite these attacks, the Turkish people were sufficiently informed to recognize that the attackers were terrorists and that refugees were victims of the same terrorists in Syria and Iraq. Had such intense terror attacks occurred in other countries in Europe, they would have mobilized a massive anti-refugee movement in society. During this period, other than a few voices, there was little demonstrable support for Türkiye's position and actions. Few outsiders cared to acknowledge the trauma that the Turkish people endured in the aftermath of these attacks, and many lacked appreciation for the understanding and hospitality of the Turkish people for the millions of refugees - as noted earlier, Türkiye leads all countries in terms of the numbers of refugees it has accepted within its borders. The plight of the refugees thus started to be considered as an issue solely about Türkiye and its international implications were neglected.

The international community's attention to the humanitarian crisis in Syria only emerged when refugees started to arrive in European countries. Prior to that, many European countries preferred not to see the humanitarian disaster and expected it to disappear on its own. The international community neglected the fact that most of the cities and towns that these refugees used to live in were destroyed and demolished by the Assad forces and thus they did not have anywhere to go back to. There was no initiative or endeavor to launch a reconstruction effort in Syria. There was also no meaningful diplomatic effort by the international community to stop the conflict in the country and guarantee a safe return of the refugees. The combined effect of these two factors made many refugees believe that it would not be possible for them to return to their homes in the foreseeable future. Now, refugees face the challenge of finding the best destination to rebuild their lives and restart their economic livelihood. While some refugees have successfully found new homes on their own, others have become unknowing prey to human smuggling networks.

There was already a network of human smugglers who operated from North Africa. Notably, the civil war in Libya forced large numbers to find safe haven on the other side of the Mediterranean Sea. Syrians who fled their cities and towns waited for years for the international community to take action to stop the atrocities of the Assad regime. Even after a chemical weapons attack, the Syrians waited for the international community to take steps to stop the bloodshed in the country. Yet, when Russia filled the power vacuum and organized operations on behalf of the Syrian regime, residents who once were committed to staying in Syria started to leave for European countries. Human smuggler networks engaged in a lucrative business in the Mediterranean and Aegean Seas, using boats to transfer Syrian refugees to the Greek islands and from there to other European countries. This scenario had the potential to create a disaster, a point the Turkish government made in raising concerns and asking for European countries to help contain the crisis along Syria's borders. Considering the legal excuses Western countries offered in denying a no-fly zone and the practical excuses they provided regarding the implementation of a safe zone for refugees, Türkiye offered its own solution. Since the rise of DAESH, most refugees left the region to save themselves and their families from violence. With countries supporting the U.S. attempts to fashion a coalition targeting DAESH, Türkiye subsequently proposed the establishment of a DAESH-free zone in the border area. Once again, the international community failed to acknowledge the potential overwhelming flow of refugee movements. The combined impact of air strikes and YPG attacks on Sunni- and Turkoman-populated cities and towns created yet another massive exodus from Syria.

European nations recognized the wave when refugees arrived from the Aegean Sea to the Greek islands. This led to a shameful moment in European history, as countries tried to stop the flow of refugees, confining them to crowded, ill-equipped detention centers and threatening force against those who resisted or defied the order of Greek authorities. In a rather short period of time, more than 300,000 refugees tried to cross the Mediterranean Sea and among them, more than 2,800 perished before reaching the coast.[10] Particularly, the Greek Coast Guard and Navy's actions to stop the refugee flow shocked the international community. Some of the boats carrying refugees were attacked by members of the coast guard to stop them from reaching the Greek islands, along with reports that Greek commandos shot at the boats to drown them.[11] Some of these attacks are well documented and have been reported by news agencies across the world.[12] Human rights organizations, such as Human Rights Watch, also confirmed these reports, with witnesses testifying that masked and armed forces played an active role in trying to push back refugees in the Aegean Sea by damaging their boats or shooting live bullets.[13] These reports along with videos that were shared on social media and picked up by international news agencies were met with little more than usual expressions of regret and condemnation, and were not backed by any substantive critical measures from the European Union toward Greece. The Greek government denied any wrongdoing,[14] and instead continued its policy of pushing back and attacking refugee boats in the Aegean Sea.

One moment that generated the greatest public outburst occurred in 2015 when photos of the body of Aylan Kurdi, a three-year-old Syrian boy, washed ashore on the Turkish coastline. The boy's family had hoped to find safe haven from DAESH in Greece, according to Greek authorities.[15] Unfortunately, their boat capsized in the middle of the sea, and the boy drowned. The image of the boy's body was shared extensively around the world on social media, generating a push for European authorities to ensure that such tragic incidents do not happen again along with fundraising campaigns to help families displaced by the civil war. Some in Europe and the U.S. started to argue that more things need to be done to help the refugees of the Syrian conflict. There were small demonstrations across Western capitals in support of a more welcoming policy towards the refugees from the war zones.

But the public outburst dissipated within a short period. One report showed that the amount of donations to the Swedish Red Cross campaign, launched in August 2015, spiked dramatically immediately after the release of the photo - moving from $3,850 to $214,300 in less than a week. But the pace of donations returned to the original meager level just six weeks later.[16] Although every penny matters in a humanitarian crisis, the incident also demonstrated why a permanent, more structured assistance plan is needed to generate sustainable mechanisms for the aid and benefit of refugees.

For those refugees who reached Greece, there were other challenges. On the islands where they are encamped, they have to endure substandard living conditions. Amnesty International has documented the circumstances, noting a scarcity of food and basic needs, and how the refugees are vulnerable to criminal acts by thugs and island residents. An Amnesty International report stated that "the hellish conditions the refugees are now forced to endure and the official indifference to their plight are appalling."[17] The crisis in Greece during this period was a problem that entailed all levels of the government in Athens. As mentioned in Amnesty International's analysis of the problem, "Local authorities in Greece are unwilling to provide the necessary assistance, national authorities appear unable to, and European leaders are dithering in the face of an ever-mounting humanitarian crisis."[18] The representative of the UNHCR in Athens also raised similar concerns about the state of refugees in these camps, telling journalists that "the situation on the islands is dramatic in terms of the sheer numbers flowing in, lack of shelter and ever worsening hygiene conditions."[19]

Later some other reports showed that the "hellish" conditions in the refugee camps had a destructive effect on the psychology of refugees. Psychologists and social workers who visited the camps in Greece reported that refugees suffered from serious psychological problems, including "post-traumatic stress disorder with acute and pervasive anxiety symptoms and major depression, with grief and loss, guilt and remorse, helplessness, and hopelessness, at times accompanied by thoughts of suicide."[20] For those who passed the Greek border to reach other European countries, the situation was not much different. A number of EU member countries treated the refugees in a way that violated basic international law conventions on human rights. When Western European countries tightened their borders to prevent an influx of refugees in their countries, many ended up being stranded in Central and Eastern European countries.

Just as with their counterparts in Western Europe, these countries were ill-prepared to handle the refugee influx given their own precarious economic conditions. They believed the best way to handle the issue was to close their borders. One country after another - Croatia, Serbia, Slovenia, and Hungary - shut their borders, leaving tens of thousands of refugees stranded in a stateless status. They traveled on foot without any food or shelter, and the weather, roads, and inhospitable environment made it extremely challenging for them to survive. One of the tragic aspects of this entire process was that the plight of the refugees took place before the cameras of international media. The media reported on nearly every move the refugees made. The world audience witnessed conditions of poverty, suffering women and children, and the use of force by border police in countries across Eastern Europe. Authorities in Eastern and Central European countries put up barbed wire, which resembled scenes of World War II concentration camps. Despite the widely circulated images and videos, the international community had yet to be moved substantially to go beyond facile expressions of sympathy to concrete humanitarian actions to ease the suffering of refugees and the burden placed on host countries.

The lack of preparation in Greece and Central and Eastern European countries was not an unresolvable problem nor an acceptable excuse. In the region, no country, including Türkiye, was prepared to handle a refugee crisis with the potential of uncertain length and scale. Türkiye had to navigate learning curves along several lines of logistics and service provisions. The government and civil society made a joint effort to help the refugees in the country. The problem for EU countries, however, was that they lacked the political will to handle the crisis. According to them, the refugees should not have been there in the first place. Goverments sent a message to refugees telling them bluntly not to come to their country.[21] Many governments contended that their countries did not have the economic capability or capacity to absorb large numbers of refugees. But there was also a more formidable issue that could not easily be resolved: anti-Muslim sentiment among certain governments complicated the manner in which the issue could be addressed strategically and tactically. Opportunistic far-right politicians presented the refugee crisis as part of an existential fight against their core national identity. For instance, some governments declared the refugees as a threat to the prosperity, security, and Christian values of Europe.[22] Some politicians even linked this refugee flow to Türkiye's policies. One of them called the refugee flow part of a grand strategy to fight Europe's Christian and Jewish roots and values. According to him, it was "a new, more sophisticated version of Turkish invasions."[23] This was a prevalent sentiment among many far-right groups in Western Europe. They successfully campaigned against accepting refugees by convincing segments of the communities, with whom they knew such perceptions would resonate, that the refugees constituted political, security, and sociocultural threats to the integrity of their national identity.

But far-right groups and nationalist governments have not been the only impediments to adequate preparations in European countries to accommodate refugees. Even those governments not hampered by far-right nationalistic groups did not act with urgency to prepare. They initially took no steps to contain the crisis in Syria and when the crisis reached their borders, they decided that the best course of action would be to seal the borders in order to block the flow of refugees. Among the ironic examples were some nations which had suffered greatly during respective civil wars in the 1990s that had forced hundreds of thousands to flee as refugees. Back then, they had also faced unwelcoming governments and communities, employment and educational discrimination in the host countries, and problems with adaptation to local cultures and routines. Now, they were on the receiving end of a refugee crisis and shut their borders.

A critical dimension of the refugee flow was the presence of multiple civil wars in the same geographical regions, and the continuous increase in the number of people who were displaced or were forced to stay in their homes for security purposes. The Syrian civil war became a classic civil war case study for the challenges of trying to respond satisfactorily to humanitarian logistical challenges. Problems were aggravated because refugees were not only coming from Syria, but also Iraq and Afghanistan, where civil wars also had become protracted.

Since the 1979 Soviet invasion of the country, Afghanistan has been a battle zone for different groups. After the U.S. invasion of Afghanistan following the 9/11 terrorist acts, hostilities persisted, and the country still lacks an environment suitable for stability and reconstruction. Now with the U.S. withdrawal from Afghanistan and the Taliban capture of large parts of the land, we have started to see a fresh wave of refugee flow from Afghanistan to Western countries, including, of course, Türkiye. When the first groups of Afghan refugees started to show up on the Turkish-Iranian border, political observers were once again not surprised by the reactions in EU countries. Some leaders expressed their opposition to receiving any refugees even before the Afghan refugees approached their borders. For instance, the chancellor of Austria expressed his opposition to accepting Afghan refugees in his country. He warned that he will continue to deport Afghans who entered Austria illegally. In addition, he claimed that several countries, including Türkiye, should be responsible for the Afghan refugees. He said, "If people are forced to flee, I think neighboring states like Türkiye or other safe parts of Afghanistan are definitely a better place than Austria, Germany, or Sweden." Of course, while saying this, Chancellor Kurz did not realize that in actual fact Türkiye is not a neighboring state of Afghanistan.[24] In 2015, Afghans constituted the second-largest group of refugees in the world.[25] However, following the rapid increase in violence in Afghanistan after the capture of parts of the country by the Taliban, the number of Afghans that flee from their country will most probably increase to a great extent.[26]

In Iraq, on the other hand, following the U.S. invasion, the civil war between different fanctions have made the country yet again a battle zone. DAESH emerged in the country in 2014 and captured major cities, leading to another series of battles between a terrorist organization and the Iraqi central government. Millions of Iraqis, vulnerable to the barbaric violence of DAESH, fled to neighboring countries. Hundreds of thousands of Iraqis headed toward Europe, only to face the conditions they encountered in previous crises. The refugee crisis in Iraq has become another long term humanitarian disaster in the world. Once again, Türkiye became the most important shelter and refuge for the Iraqis who fled from the region. As President Erdoğan put it succinctly, "At a time when the world's most developed nations shut their doors on oppressed people, running from war, starvation, and terrorism, Türkiye welcomed millions of asylum seekers from Syria and Iraq, regardless of their ethnicity, language, or religious affiliation."[27]

Türkiye's warning to the EU and other countries around the world to contain this crisis and share the burden did not receive a substantive positive response. In September 2015, then UN refugee chief António Guterres offered recommendations to the EU on how to manage the crisis, which differed very little from what Türkiye had undertaken on its own. He asked European countries not to consider this as a migration issue while reminding them that the refugees were running for their lives from conflict zones in Syria, Iraq, and Afghanistan. He reiterated that the issue is too big to be resolved by one single state, arguing that a common strategy, joint efforts, and solidarity among European countries is necessary.[28] It took a while for European institutions to take charge and negotiate with Türkiye to solve the problem. In the end, the deal that the EU signed with Türkiye after this crisis could not resolve the concerns because the EU did not fulfill its side of the agreement.

Europe's failure in handling the refugee crisis reverberated with consequences. While the wealthy European countries failed to help resolve the crisis, other countries in the crisis regions faced grim circumstances due to the lack of resources and capacity. As of 2020, countries including Pakistan, Sudan, Lebanon, and Bangladesh are among the top ten hosts of refugees, mostly with limited support from the international community. The continuation of conflict, disputes, and the persecution of people alongside their borders make these countries a destination for the displaced people of different countries, including Afghans and the Rohingya people of Myanmar. Yemen has been a complicated case for the last five years. Since the beginning of the proxy war, according to data provided by the UNHCR, almost 3.8 million people have had to leave their homes. The displacement continues today as the conflict between different factions has made it impossible for Yemenis to live in their country. However, Yemen has also received a significant number of refugees from countries like Somalia. Dating to the 1980s, there have been different waves of refugee flows to Yemen from Somalia. Following the beginning of the civil war in their country, more Somalians arrived in Yemen because of the fear of persecution and violence as well as the lack of opportunities to sustain their livelihood. Their numbers surpassed 200,000.[29] Thus, when the civil war broke out and people were displaced in Yemen, the country was already hosting a sizable refugee population. This generated dire circumstances for the refugees in the country and the burgeoning numbers of internally displaced people. Today, according to UN data, 80 percent of the people in the country require urgent humanitarian assistance.[30] The war has destroyed Yemen's already crippled economy. Statistics show that two-thirds of the population in the country cannot afford food, a situation that has brought many Yemenis on the edge of starvation.[31] The shortage of food is not the only problem. As the civil war in the country entered its fifth year, significant health risks became an emergency given the rapid spread of cholera and diphtheria. The lack of proper health care and clean water have made these outbreaks more deadly for the Yemenis. But, as with other cases, the attention and assistance of the international community once again has proven to be insufficient.

The Failure of the International Community in Development Assistance

The failure of the international system has not only been felt in the refugee crisis but also in the economic state of the least developed and developing countries. Repeated warnings from humanitarian aid organizations and calls from socially conscious and socially responsible influential voices did not compel the international community to respond more effectively and comprehensively. In every instance, there were warning signs about impending humanitarian crises and numerous red flags for the international community that inaction would lead to a catastrophe which would be difficult to manage properly and from which it would be hard to recover. In some instances, these inequalities and lack of opportunities have contributed to other refugee crises. Particularly following the 2008 financial meltdown, advanced economies around the world acted first to save themselves from the global recession while neglecting countries that felt the crisis but had no instrumental means to handle it.

According to statistics and the reports of international institutions, overall, there is a decline in the poverty rate around the world, but in recent years this decline has slowed dramatically. According to the World Bank, more than 730 million live in extreme poverty and are struggling to meet their most basic needs such as education, health care, and access to sanitation and water. The rate of poverty is extremely high for low-income countries, and those affected by conflict and political upheaval.[32] For instance, according to the World Bank, the conflicts in Yemen and Syria have expanded the overall poverty level in the Middle East and North Africa.[33] In another region of the African continent, the presence of extreme poverty persists. Sub-Saharan Africa now accounts for the majority of poor people in the world. Despite the poverty rate decline in most regions, the number of poor people is increasing in this region. Among the 28 poorest countries of the world, 27 of them are located in sub-Saharan Africa.[34] The international community has failed to attend to the deteriorating condition in the region's states. The lack of action also aggravates tensions of inequality within the same region between countries, and within the same country between different classes. The worsening situation in sub-Saharan Africa makes it extremely challenging for the World Bank and other institutions to meet the 2030 goals regarding poverty reduction.

This inequality between regions is also visible in other metrics of development. The data shows that sub-Saharan Africa is far behind the desired objectives and numbers. For instance, in regard to child mortality rate, sub-Saharan Africa has the highest rate of child mortality. According to the data provided by the World Bank, the child mortality rate in these regions is 10 percent, meaning that one in every ten children dies before reaching the age of five.[35] According to the World Health Organization (WHO), the risk of infant mortality in the region is six times higher than in Europe.[36] Once again, just like the poverty rate, the child mortality rate is also significantly related to the presence of active conflict in a country or a region. Following sub-Saharan Africa, the countries that have the highest child mortality rate are engulfed in civil wars: Yemen, Syria, Afghanistan, and Myanmar.[37] It is true that the world as a whole is still far from the objectives set forth in the Sustainable Development Goals by the UN. The UN set out to bring down the rate of child mortality to 2.5 percent globally. Although there were significant reductions in some parts of the world, is far behind the criteria established by the UN. Today, the rate of child mortality is 3.9 percent globally and approximately 15,000 children die every day.[38]

In other metrics the picture is not much different. There is significant development in the world with regard to some criteria, such as access to education, drinking water, and sanitation services. But also, some regions have been left significantly behind in these metrics. There has not been systematic aid and assistance to save these countries and nations from this underdevelopment trap. The international system does not provide the means to help those who have been left behind in development. For instance, the WHO/UNICEF Joint Monitoring Programme (JMP) confirms that 2.1 billion people are not able to access safe drinking water services and almost half of the world population still does not receive sanitation services.[39] The report published by WHO/UNICEF has shown a similar trend in these metrics revealing that "1.8 billion people have gained access to basic drinking water services since 2000, but there are vast inequalities in the accessibility, availability and quality of these services. It is estimated that 1 in 10 people in the world still lack basic services, including the 144 million who drink untreated surface water."[40]

These are massive inequalities that have led to significant health crises and further refugee and migration crises in these countries. Especially considering the COVID-19 pandemic, the data provided a rather bleak picture about future pandemics and the precautions that nations are expected to take to prevent a high degree of casualties. The report demonstrates that in 2017, approximately 3 billion people lacked basic hand-washing facilities with soap and water at home. The situation is much worse when looking at less developed countries. According to the data in the same report, nearly 75 percent of the population in the world's least developed countries does not have basic hand-washing facilities.[41] This inequality regarding access to sanitation in the world generates significant gaps and differences during epidemics. Sanitation access has been a major cause of the rapid emergence and spread of certain diseases in underdeveloped countries. According to the data, due to the lack of access to sanitation, every year almost 300,000 children die from diarrhea. Accordingly, lack of sanitation has also contributed to the rapid spread of diseases such as cholera, dysentery, hepatitis A, and typhoid.[42] And, as in other crises, the assistance from the international community has not adequately responded to these needs. Major initiatives such as the Millennium Development Goals or the Sustainable Development Goals will become less effective if the international community does not back them with material support and concrete resources.

It is important to remember that the inequalities in the development level of countries do not only cause misery and poverty for citizens, but their impacts easily spread across borders, triggering waves of destabilization. The poverty rate, declining quality of life, and malnutrition coupled with poor governance and weak state institutions carry effects such as triggering a refugee crisis, straining economic resources, social tensions, exporting of insecurity, the failure to contain epidemics, and the danger of becoming a center for smuggling and crimnal networks. The advanced economies in the world must attend to fortifying the culture of interdependence in the global community if they are to suppress and mitigate conditions that otherwise threaten to destabilize whole regions and worsen economic conditions even where countries have finally achieved sustainable development. The international system should be motivated to develop mechanisms of solidarity in order to handle crises arising from the causes discussed above. The burden must be shared fairly among the advanced economies in order to achieve a sustainable program of development assistance. Short-term assistance and inadequate planning can only function as bandages that cannot repel the hemorrhaging effects of crises, which can quickly cascade across borders and contested territories.

The COVID-19 Pandemic

The value of networked connections and interdependence became obvious during the COVID-19 pandemic. At the height of the first and second waves of cases, economies were shut down and cities were placed under lockdowns in every region of the world. The epicenter of the disease shifted from Asia to Europe in early 2020 and later traveled across North America, Latin America, and Southeast Asia. The outbreak reminded people around the world that humanity is united by a shared destiny. The travel bans, curfews, and border restrictions could not stop the virus from reaching every corner of the world. With one virus, the world came to a halt and political and diplomatic interactions between countries went dormant for the period. It is the worst pandemic the world has faced since the influenza outbreak in 1918. It soon became clear that the international system had not developed mechanisms to cope with such outbreaks. Political, economic, and strategic issues overshadowed public health problems across the world. Institutions, such as the World Health Organization, and health agencies in highly advanced economies moved forward to manage the pandemic but at the same time, the lack of a central force in the international system led to inequalities and discrepancies in accessing health care and health services. The outbreak exacerbated already existing poverty levels and the lack of opportunities in the least developed countries. As mentioned above, even before the pandemic, some countries had a hard time accessing means of sanitation. Billions of people, according to this data, do not possess simple soap and running water to wash their hands, as was directed to do in order to minimize the transmission risk of the coronavirus. Furthermore, people did not have access to masks, personal protection equipment, and other types of sanitizers to curb the spread. In fact, initially it was thought that some of these less-developed regions of the world could avoid the first wave of the pandemic due to the decreased international mobility of the people living there. At the end of April 2020, the WHO data showed that the least developed countries represented a small fraction of the cases in the world: all of these countries combined had 0.56 percent of global cases and 0.23 percent of global deaths.[43] Soon after, many realized that the low numbers were not a result of the lack of infection but instead of the lack of testing capabilities.[44]

Other measures advised by the WHO and other public health agencies have also been difficult to adopt in the least developed countries, especially where active civil wars or weak state institutions make it difficult to shut down the economy and enforce lockdowns. Practicing social distancing has also not been feasible in refugee camps.[45] Reports indicate that even with the implementation of these measures, these countries would still face a severe magnitude of existing inequalities. Fragile health systems in these countries are further strained by a large number of COVID-19 cases. Some of these countries were already suffering from significant outbreaks of other illnesses even before the emergence of COVID-19, including malaria, HIV/AIDS, and tuberculosis. Some countries were just recovering from other epidemics, such as Ebola, when COVID-19 hit the region. The UN's chief concern revolved around the diversion of critical resources, in addition to long periods of malnutrition that had already compromised the overall health condition of individuals in least developed countries.[46] The lack of medical equipment, including personal protective equipment, affected the capacity of health-care workers to address the pandemic. Furthermore, the global demand for ventilators and other medical equipment shut out these countries from accessing the supply, as every country prioritized its own efforts for the benefit of its citizens. This led to major shortages in imported materials and incoming donations from different organizations and charities.

In much of 2020, prolonged lockdowns burdened the global economy and triggered supply slowdowns in moving essential goods. Many countries experienced a rapid rise in unemployment and decline in the GDP per capita. The outbreak particularly impacted already fragile economies in less developed countries, where loss of income through tourism and other service sectors generated high levels of unemployment. The precarious state of the economy in these countries also hobbled their capacity to enact substantial relief packages to stimulate and revitalize their economies while covering services for health care and public welfare. The pandemic sharpened the distinction for those countries already hampered by systematic inequalities. In advanced economies, such as the U.S., there were also sharper distinctions of inequity, drawn along class and race lines. For example, while African Americans constitute 13 percent of the population, more than 19 percent of the people who were hospitalized were African American. A similar disproportionate situation was also present for Hispanics in the United States.[47] According to the U.S. Centers for Disease Control, the source of the disproportionate situation stems from different reasons, including systematic discrimination of ethnic and racial groups in the public health sector, and inequality of health-care access and utilization, education, wealth, and housing.[48] In addition to the inequalities being sharpened within advanced economies, inequality on a global level also became more visible as a result of the COVID-19 pandemic. Unfortunately, there were virtually no institutional mechanisms to coordinate a response that would have mitigated the sharpness of inequality for the most vulnerable least or less developed countries.

This was certainly the case for countries engulfed in civil wars and lesser conflicts. According to a report on northwestern Syria published by the United Nations Office for the Coordination of Humanitarian Affairs (OCHA), "Despite the decrease in hostilities in the region due to the March 6 cease-fire, humanitarian needs for nearly 4 million people remain severe."[49] The Britain-based Syrian Observatory for Human Rights stated that the humanitarian situation in northwestern Syria was already dire and as the pandemic spread, a catastrophic scenario would emerge for the Syrian people.[50] However, the international community's efforts did not even provide necessary humanitarian aid for people's basic needs. The situation in Idlib continued to worsen during the pandemic.[51] Humanitarian organizations such as the White Helmets announced that the situation could lead to another major humanitarian disaster in the midst of an already existing one.[52] The situation in refugee camps proved to be more challenging than ever. In October 2020, it was reported that there was a tenfold increase in the infection numbers in the refugee camps in Idlib.[53] This coincided with the world enduring a second wave of infection, much more deadly than the first which triggered the global lockdowns. Yet, for refugees, the story unfortunately was the same - pandemic or no pandemic.

Scientists immediately converged on finding vaccines, with multiple efforts occurring around the world. Due to the hard work of different scientists globally, in a rather short period of time, multiple companies produced vaccines to combat COVID-19. One question that was not immediately answered was how universal access to the vaccine would be facilitated. Before the end of 2020, vaccines became available in advanced economies, while researchers were concerned that less developed countries might wait a year or longer to gain access to them. Of course, rollout of shots entailed addressing the cost and availability as well as logistical issues like transportation and storage facilities. Some of these vaccines needed to be kept in cold storage for transportation and inventory purposes. In 2021, as the pandemic eased in advanced economies, some of the worst outbreaks of the disease, including more easily transmissible variants of the virus, occurred in countries with the most limited access to vaccines and where vaccination rates were among the lowest. There was a significant gap in the numbers of available vaccines in different countries around the world. Especially in the least developed countries, there was a significant shortage in accessing vaccines. This major gap did not only pose a significant risk for the people in the least developed countries but also to the state of the COVID-19 pandemic globally. Researchers warned of a significant risk to large segments of unvaccinated populations in areas that do not achieve an effective level of herd immunity.[54]

Solidarity and cooperation between countries have not been present during the COVID-19 crisis. Similar to the international community's response to other humanitarian crises, the role of international institutions during the pandemic has been disappointing from the perspective of underdeveloped countries. Perpetuating pessimism vis-à-vis globalization and international cooperation, nation-states resisted opportunities for cooperation or coordination. Instead, systems predicated on self-dependence largely prevailed at the international level. As mentioned previously, the World Health Organization was the first international institution that failed to respond adequately to the pandemic. The failure was compounded by the lack of interest among states to reform and bolster institutions that would become essential. In the U.S., the Trump administration decided to suspend its funding to the organization amid the pandemic instead of expanding its engagement to reconcile grievances and directly address the pandemic concerns. The EU fell short of even acknowledging the gravity of the pandemic in its member states, particularly during the earliest stages of the outbreak. It left member states to fend for themselves, even with items as simple as masks and personal protective equipment. The lack of assistance that Italy and Spain received in the first months of the pandemic led to a rapid spread of the virus and the failure of health care systems to contain the crisis. Calls for assistance to fight the pandemic by member states were not answered revealing the lack of unity within the union. Italian Prime Minister Giuseppe Conte stated that "if Europe does not rise to this unprecedented challenge, the whole European structure loses its raison d'être to the people. We are at a critical point in European history."[55] European Commission President Ursula von der Leyen also criticized the member states that had ceased sending medical equipment to other nations and only considered their own national interest.[56]

Türkiye's Humanitarian Policy

Türkiye's experience in handling humanitarian crises was developed initially by its willingness and capacity to host the largest share of refugees in the world. Since the beginning of the civil war in 2011, the government's humanitarian priorities in its foreign policy facilitated an "open door" approach for Syrians, without exerting ethnic or religious discrimination. To reiterate, currently Türkiye hosts more than 5 million refugees including 3.9 million Syrians and 500,000 asylum seekers and refugees of other nationalities, including individuals from Iran, Iraq, Somalia, and Afghanistan.[57] Especially after the beginning of the U.S. withdrawal from Afghanistan, there is a massive flow of refugees from Afghanistan to different countries in the region. The data on this massive, new flow has demonstrated that one of the most significant destinations for these refugees is Türkiye. Türkiye's humanitarian assistance to refugees is not limited to these countries. As it is a transit destination for many migrants hoping to reach European countries, Eritrean, Bangladeshi, Pakistani, Moroccan, Algerian, Syrian, and Afghan nationals try to enter Türkiye.

In this crisis, Türkiye has filled a gap left unattended by its European peers. In addition to accepting those who fled from Syria, the Turkish government and aid agencies also launched major humanitarian initiatives for the internally displaced peoples in Syria, particularly in the northwestern portions of the country. This includes Idlib, where nearly 4 million internally displaced peoples found themselves in dire living conditions. After attacks by air forces of the Syrian regime and its allies in the region, almost a million people were forced from their homes and moved towards the Turkish border. One of the largest makeshift refugee camps was formed in the northern part of the region bordering Türkiye. As reported by journalists and camp residents the situation can be extremely dire in this area. But, as before, there has not been sufficient international assistance. Aid campaigns, which intended to build shelters for the internally displaced people, were launched by civil society organizations and the Turkish government, and provided some degree of relief for these Syrians.[58] The Turkish Red Crescent also launched efforts to provide temporary housing for the affected people.[59] Humanitarian assistance from the UN and other international organizations has always been welcome, but it is insufficient in alleviating the plight of refugees in the region, given the numbers involved.

It is ironic that the international community is aware of Türkiye's sacrifices in handling the refugee crisis. Türkiye has been lauded by many officials from international organizations for its endeavors to aid refugees. Katharina Lumpp, the UN High Commission for Refugees' representative in Türkiye, said, "It's always been a few countries that host very large numbers of refugees, and Türkiye's response has been exemplary."[60] Lumpp added, "Türkiye embraced a very comprehensive and legal framework for foreigners and for international protection." In addition, she criticized the international community by arguing that it should not only focus on responding to the humanitarian needs of refugees, but also support host countries and communities because it is the host countries that endure the responsibility on behalf of the international community.[61] Lumpp also praised Türkiye's harmonization and inclusive policies for refugees in terms of the social interaction between Turkish citizens and refugees. Although Türkiye has been hosting larger refugee populations than other countries, it provides better standards for refugees when compared to camps in Western countries. The camps have operated to ensure education, health care, and essential infrastructure are available.

Turkey has also led many countries around the world in terms of humanitarian assistance. According to the Global Humanitarian Assistance Report by the Development Initiative (DI), Türkiye was in the lead in expenditures for global humanitarian assistance in 2017 and 2018. While Türkiye spent $8.1 billion in 2017, its humanitarian assistance expenses grew to $8.4 billion in 2018.[62] On the other hand, the U.S., Germany, and the UK with larger GDP impacts, followed Türkiye with $6.65 billion, $2.97 billion, and $2.20 billion, respectively. In

2018, Türkiye's humanitarian assistance expenses were approximately 1.1% of its GDP, up from 1% in 2017, while the U.S. supplied 0.032% of its GDP, Germany 0.074%, and the UK 0.077%.[63]

Later, when a pandemic hit the globe and caused countries to downgrade their humanitarian policies, the Turkish government decided not to change its approach to the humanitarian crises in its southern border. Although in many parts of the world, refugees faced additional challenges following the COVID-19 outbreak, Türkiye's humanitarian efforts have not been curtailed or sidelined during the pandemic. Similarly, the economic crisis during the COVID-19 pandemic caused many countries around the world to calibrate their budget and cut their humanitarian assistance programs. However, Ankara did the opposite and continued its exemplary humanitarian assistance programs during this period.

The failure of the international community to address different humanitarian crises was not limited to the crises in the Middle East. In different parts of the world, humanitarian tragedies emerged because of civil wars and suppressive policies of authoritarian regimes. Türkiye, under the leadership of Erdoğan, tried to help refugees and people in need in different parts of the world during these crises. For instance, the grave circumstances affecting the Rohingya people, who have seen their basic human rights stripped in Myanmar and placed under siege by that nation's military forces, compelled Türkiye to activate humanitarian efforts to ease their suffering.[64] Türkiye has remained at the forefront of providing humanitarian assistance to Rohingya refugees who escaped from Myanmar to Bangladesh. Turkish institutions, including the Turkish Cooperation and Coordination Agency (TIKA), the Turkish Red Crescent, Türkiye Diyanet Foundation, and the Disaster and Emergency Management Authority (AFAD) contributed assistance to the persecuted Rohingya by providing daily meals, shelter, and health care to tens of thousands of people. Turkish government officials at the highest level visited the refugee camps in Bangladesh and promised to alleviate any problems there. In addition, the Turkish government has tried to raise awareness about the topic and bring the issue of Rohingya Muslims to the agenda of the UN and other international organizations. Türkiye has called on the international community to contribute to aid efforts for the Rohingya people. President Erdoğan during his addresses to the UN General Assembly has asked the international community to take steps to alleviate the condition of the Rohingya people. However, once again, the international community has failed to act effectively to address this crisis.[65]

The Turkish government has also attempted to extend its assistance to the people of Yemen, who have endured more than six years of civil war. Many essential services have stopped in the country, most of the infrastructure has been destroyed, and more than half of the country's population is trying to survive with foreign aid. Türkiye is one of the biggest donors providing humanitarian assistance to the war-torn country. It supports the peace efforts for resolving the Yemeni conflict by promoting inclusive dialogue and sending humanitarian aid to the country. More recently, TIKA, AFAD, the Yemen High Relief Committee, and the relevant provincial governorates delivered 3,000 food parcels to families in need in the Yemeni provinces of Taiz and Lahij.[66]

Amplifying an earlier point, Türkiye has set the pace for humanitarian assistance. The amount of development assistance it has provided to various countries around the world reached $9.33 billion in 2017 and $9.93 billion in 2018.[67] Türkiye has become the sixth highest-ranking country in providing development assistance, overtaking many developed countries like the U.S., the United Kingdom, France, and Germany.[68] Countries benefiting most from the official development assistance of Türkiye include Syria, Kyrgyzstan, Kazakhstan, Afghanistan, Somalia, Palestine, and Sudan. Türkiye has also provided the highest official development assistance to Syria, amounting to $6.7 billion in 2018.[69]

The role of the Turkish people in this process is also important. The Turkish government could not provide this level of assistance to other countries without public consent or approval. In addition to providing public support, the Turkish public also acts proactively to help those in need. Apart from official development assistance, Türkiye has provided development assistance to developing countries through direct investments by the private sector and NGOs. Charity groups and civil society organizations have been mobilized to raise money for those in dire conditions in different parts of the world. The Turkish government has adopted a plan to contribute to developing countries in disadvantaged regions by transmitting Türkiye's experience, and promoting fair and sustainable cooperation based on mutual trust.[70] The Turkish government considers the priorities and needs of countries by acknowledging and being sensitive to the respective local culture and national values.[71]

There are various examples of modern, tangible, and sustainable projects organized by Turkish development agencies. They have implemented more than 140 projects for 900,000 people in health care, and have trained approximately 5,000 doctors, civil servants, and experts.[72] They have also brought to fruition nearly 4,250 projects in the education field and constructed schools in countries on four continents, including in Afghanistan, Albania, Cambodia, Ethiopia, Palestine, Iraq, and Colombia.[73] In addition, Turkish agencies have launched initiatives to drill hundreds of water wells in Africa,[74] providing clean water to 1.8 million people living in Niger, Mali, Burkina Faso, Mauritania, Somalia, and Somaliland.[75] By providing development assistance to various countries, Türkiye also indirectly contributes to these states' development of functioning institutions. For instance, Türkiye is the main contributor of development assistance to Somalia and has helped it achieve a new, sustainable structure by donating approximately $1 billion.[76]

Türkiye has demonstrated similar solidarity during the coronavirus pandemic by delivering medical aid to various countries and opening diplomatic channels to reinforce a spirit of cooperation during the public health crisis. While many countries adopted protectionist measures in regard to the transfer of medical equipment to other countries, Türkiye followed a different path and decided to share its supplies with those in dire need in the midst of the pandemic. From the very beginning, Türkiye believes that without a global effort it will be impossible to control the spread of COVID-19 and put a stop to the pandemic. Individual and selfish efforts would backfire and only contribute to the prolongation of the pandemic. Two-thirds of the countries in the world have requested help from Türkiye during the pandemic, and 80 have received cargo planes carrying medical supplies.[77] Türkiye sent medical supplies to the countries that were most affected by the coronavirus pandemic, including China, Iran, Iraq, the UK, Ireland, and the United States.[78]

What to Do Next

In the last several decades, the refugee issue has reached unprecedented levels of occurrence and persistence, signaling the most extensive humanitarian disaster since World War II. The flow of refugees has not only endangered the lives of the refugees, but has also threatened to destabilize the hosting nations and communities. Although poverty reduction programs have been deemed successful in most countries, hundreds of millions around the world remain paralyzed by dire economic and social conditions. The COVID-19 outbreak demonstrated that pandemics can pose varying magnitudes of threats to different countries depending on their development status. Although most of the heavily impacted countries seem to be among the developed countries of the world. There is also uncertainty about the level of damage that the pandemic has exacted on the health, economy, and security of less developed countries. The pandemic has demonstrated that countries around the world are left to fend for themselves, an unfortunate fact that has become far too common as a strategic preference. Already, experts not just in medicine and science but also economists, political scientists, and others emphasize that a failure to enact interdependent policies will aggravate and deepen existing social and economic inequalities across the world. Considering the potential inequalities in vaccine distribution and implementation already witnessed, it is believed that broader existing inequalities will be sharpened in the post-pandemic recovery.

The international system that was established after the end of World War II and was expected to bring peace and stability to the entire world has failed persistently to find a sustainable solution to people's suffering. Although there are constant calls to protect the international system, maintaining the status quo will bring little, if any, improvements to existing humanitarian challenges. In order to alleviate the humanitarian condition, the system must be reformed to prioritize humanitarian efforts as a worthy investment with mutual aid approaches. For the last two decades, Türkiye has set a worthwhile example to encourage the international community to establish global cooperation and coordination to respond more effectively to humanitarian crises. Türkiye, for numerous reasons, has become the country that hosts the highest number of refugees. Türkiye moved into the top tier of countries that provide development assistance to other countries. During the pandemic, Türkiye was again among the countries that provided the highest amount of aid to countries in need. Türkiye has demonstrated that these humanitarian challenges are not insurmountable, but can be resolved through a consistent and holistic approach.

Türkiye's actions underscore the value of enabling and empowering regional and national networks to address these crises instead of taking a competition-driven approach that allows countries to detach and even ignore addressing the most critical dimensions of humanitarian policy responses. Resolving this begins with a strategy that asks existing humanitarian institutional bureaucracies to reform and engage more collegially with newcomers in humanitarian policy who have focused on pandemic and health care issues, the climate crisis, chronic violence in communities, and war technologies that have prolonged and protracted conflicts. No single country can manage such crises unilaterally. Therefore, it would be not only unfair but also unrealistic and unsustainable to leave global problems, such as the refugee problems, to some countries.

It is completely unfathomable that Syria, Yemen or any other country facing a humanitarian disaster due to an active civil war can rebuild its country on its own or even with the support of one or a handful of neighboring countries. There also must be more constructive discussions about how the global community should assist countries in appropriately addressing ethnic and religious tensions before allowing them to erupt into full-scale violence and the ensuing refugee crisis that comes with such hostilities. Simply, efforts must operate in parallel to resolve conflicts and address the needs and welfare of refugees dislocated by hostilities. The foreign policy teams of nation-states should advocate for and invite donors (i.e., humanitarian institutions) to work with national and local governments, regional geopolitical institutions, religious and civil society organizations, trade unions, and mutual aid organizations dedicated to health care on both a strategic and tactical basis. International organizations should be supported, and their funding needs should be satisfied. Options should include providing a safe zone for internally displaced peoples, deterring military forces from attacking civilians, compiling necessary humanitarian aid, and providing a safe passage of assistance to those in need. The countries in the region that may have to host the exodus without a safe zone should be supported in this process, both financially and in terms of security. Burden-sharing should start from the beginning and depending on the development of the situation on the ground, international institutions and other countries should be prepared to extend other forms of assistance to help refugees. Food, shelter, and medical assistance would only be initial and short term. Considering how conflicts become protracted, other forms of refugee assistance should encompass temporary relocation, education, and other logistical considerations. Operating and managing refugee camps entails a complex operation akin to establishing a functioning city within a matter of days: public health services, education and instruction, security, and public safety, economic-related services including training and matriculation into the job market. There should be aggressive enforcement to deter criminal syndicates and smuggling networks, carried out along the lines of a protocol and code crafted through transnational cooperation and coordination.

Progress toward eliminating extreme poverty is and has been a commendable objective, but the issue remains that such efforts require a longer-term perspective than what is available presently. There is a regional imbalance in the performance of poverty reduction rates, so a more comprehensive, fair, equitable approach is needed. Data demonstrate that poverty has expanded in some areas, such as sub-Saharan Africa. In areas where internal conflicts and civil wars occur, poverty rates might be entrenched to the point that solutions demand a longitudinal perspective. COVID-19 has illuminated just how vital public health and welfare responses are, including ensuring access to basic medical services and sufficient equipment and devices to deal with epidemics. Public health care service delivery is crucial to sustaining and protecting economies because if they fail, millions of people in the affected country are vulnerable to exploitation and corruption by government officials and businesses that have no interest in humanitarian or altruistic purposes.

Türkiye supports the Sustainable Development Goals framework in aiding efforts to eradicate poverty in the world. It also advocates for a more feasible, flexible strategy to diversify and expand contributions that can adequately shift the resources in case of a humanitarian disaster or underdevelopment due to external factors, such as civil war and natural disaster, and ensure their fair distribution. Türkiye also supports the end goal of development assistance to make countries ultimately self-dependent economically. To achieve the goal of sustainability, the effort of one country is insufficient. Both developed nations and developing nations should encourage parallel and mutual efforts to gain the cooperation of public and private enterprises and NGOs.

The recommendations suggest reforming international infrastructure beyond short-term patchwork and inviting more diverse arrangements of nation-states to collaborate on humanitarian efforts. The COVID-19 pandemic confirmed the deficiencies in the existing system, mainly because the effects of lockdowns and business shutdowns affected all countries, regardless of where they stood in development status. The impact was enough to accelerate what had been already diminishing returns in the viability of the existing international order, thereby further eroding public trust and confidence in the system. Many countries have adopted plans outlining a vision of objectives to be achieved by 2030. Within this time framework, every country could add the objective of reforming and repurposing humanitarian institutions, while inviting new players and enterprising approaches that acknowledge the 21st-century shifts in geopolitical realities.

ENDNOTES

1 Erdoğan, Recep Tayyip, *A Fairer World Is Possible: A Proposed Model for United Nations Reform*, Istanbul, September 2021.

2 Ibid., p. 6.

3 Altun, Fahrettin, "11 Eylül Literatürü ve Bizden Neden Nefret Ediyorlar Sorusu Üzerine," *Tezkire*, Year: 10, No: 25, March/April 2002, pp. 32-51.

4 Ibid., p. 20

5 Ibid., p. 31.

6 See the report by Amnesty International, 2019, "Afghanistan's Refugees: Forty Years of Dispossession," n.d., https://www.amnesty.org/en/latest/news/2019/06/Afghanistan-refugees-forty-years/.

7 "Figures at a Glance," UNHCR, The UN Refugee Agency, n.d., retrieved May 16, 2020, https://www.unhcr.org/figures-at-a-glance.html.

8 "COVID-19 Threatens Refugee Camps," n.d., International Rescue Committee (IRC), https://www.rescue.org/covid-19-threatens-refugee-camps.

9 "Four Things to Know about Covid in the World's Largest Refugee Camp," Oxfam International, March 11, 2021, https://www.oxfam.org/en/blogs/four-things-know-about-covid-worlds-largest-refugee-camp.

10 Clayton, J, "UNHCR Chief Issues Key Guidelines for Dealing with Europe's Refugee Crisis," UNHCR, September 4, 2015, https://www.unhcr.org/news/latest/2015/9/55e9793b6/unhcr-chief-issues-key-guidelines-dealing-europes-refugee-crisis.html.

11 Jones, Sophia, "Masked 'Commandos' Are Attacking Refugee Boats off This Idyllic Greek Island," Huffington Post, August 13, 2015, https://www.huffpost.com/entry/greek-migrant-boats-attacked_n_55cbabf1e4b0898c488664e6.

12 CBS Evening News, Boats from Greece Confront Refugees at Sea with Guns, n.d., https://www.youtube.com/watch?v=7w0OpYG3Om8.

13 "Greece: Attacks on Boats Risk Migrant Lives," Human Rights Watch, October 22, 2015, https://www.hrw.org/news/2015/10/22/greece-attacks-boats-risk-migrant-lives.

14 Ibid.

15 "Shocking Images of Drowned Syrian Boy Show Tragic Plight of Refugees," *The Guardian*, September 2, 2015, http://www.theguardian.com/world/2015/sep/02/shocking-image-of-drowned-syrian-boy-shows-tragic-plight-of-refugees.

16 Slovic, Paul, Daniel Västfjäll, Arvid Erlandsson, and Robin Gregory, "Iconic Photographs and the Ebb and Flow of Empathic Response to Humanitarian Disasters," *Proceedings of the National Academy of Sciences* 114 (4): 640-44, 2017, https://doi.org/10.1073/pnas.1613977114.

17 "Greece: Refugees Attacked and in 'Hellish Conditions' on Kos," Amnesty International, September 4, 2015, https://www.amnesty.org/en/latest/news/2015/09/greece-refugees-attacked-and-in-hellish-conditions-on-kos/.

18 Ibid.

19 "Shocking Images of Drowned Syrian Boy Show Tragic Plight of Refugees," *The Guardian*, September 2, 2015, http://www.theguardian.com/world/2015/sep/02/shocking-image-of-drowned-syrian-boy-shows-tragic-plight-of-refugees.

20 Connelly, Andrew, "Refugees Suffer PTSD and Attempt Suicide in Greece," The World from PRX, April 10, 2017, https://www.pri.org/stories/2017-04-10/refugees-suffer-ptsd-and-attempt-suicide-greece.

21 Bilefsky, Dan, "17,000 Migrants Stranded in Croatia by Border Crackdown," *The New York Times*, September 18, 2015, sec. World, https://www.nytimes.com/2015/09/19/world/europe/refugee-migrant-crisis-europe.html.

22 Reuters in Berkasovo, "More Than 10,000 Refugees Stranded in Serbia as Borders Close, UNHCR Says," *The Guardian*, October 19, 2015, http://www.theguardian.com/world/2015/oct/19/refugees-stranded-on-serbian-croatian-border.

23 Bilefsky, Dan, "17,000 Migrants Stranded in Croatia by Border Crackdown," *The New York Times*, September 18, 2015, sec. World, https://www.nytimes.com/2015/09/19/world/europe/refugee-migrant-crisis-europe.html.

24 Bathke, Benjamin, "Austrian Chancellor Warns of New Refugee Flows, Says Deportations to Afghanistan Will Continue," InfoMigrants, July 26, 2021. https://www.infomigrants.net/en/post/33865/austrian-chancellor-warns-of-new-refugee-flows-says-deportations-to-Afghanistan-will-continue.

25 "Migrant Crisis: Migration to Europe Explained in Seven Charts," BBC News, March 4, 2016, sec. Europe, https://www.bbc.com/news/world-europe-34131911.

26 Bathke, "Austrian Chancellor Warns of New Refugee Flows."

27 Erdoğan, *A Fairer World Is Possible*, p. 23.

28 Clayton, J., "UNHCR Chief Issues Key Guidelines for Dealing with Europe's Refugee Crisis," UNHCR, September 4, 2015, https://www.unhcr.org/news/latest/2015/9/55e9793b6/unhcr-chief-issues-key-guidelines-dealing-europes-refugee-crisis.html.

29 "Amid Worsening Conditions in Yemen, More Somali Refugees Opt to Return," UNHCR, May 31, 2019, https://www.unhcr.org/news/briefing/2019/5/5cf0e7eb4/amid-worsening-conditions-yemen-somali-refugees-opt-return.html.

30 "Yemen Refugee Crisis: Aid, Statistics and News | USA for UNHCR," n.d., https://www.unrefugees.org/emergencies/yemen/.

31 Ibid.

32 "Decline of Global Extreme Poverty Continues but Has Slowed," World Bank,

September 19, 2018, https://www.worldbank.org/en/news/press-release/2018/09/19/decline-of-global-extreme-poverty-continues-but-has-slowed-world-bank.

33 Ibid.

34 "Poverty and Shared Prosperity 2018," World Bank, n.d., https://www.worldbank.org/en/publication/poverty-and-shared-prosperity-2018.

35 Roser, Max, Hannah Ritchie, and Bernadeta Dadonaite, "Child and Infant Mortality," *Our World in Data,* May, https://ourworldindata.org/child-mortality.

36 "Global Health Observatory Data."

37 Roser, Ritchie, and Dadonaite, "Child and Infant Mortality."

38 Ibid.

39 "Progress on Household Drinking Water, Sanitation and Hygiene 2000-2017," June 14, 2019, https://www.who.int/publications-detail-redirect/9789241516235.

40 Osseiran, Nada, and Yemi Lufadeju, "1 in 3 People Globally Do Not Have Access to Safe Drinking Water – UNICEF, WHO," June 18, 2019, https://www.who.int/news/item/18-06-2019-1-in-3-people-globally-do-not-have-access-to-safe-drinking-water-unicef-who.

41 Ibid.

42 Ibid.

43 "COVID-19 and the Least Developed Countries | Department of Economic and Social Affairs," 2020, May 1, 2020, https://www.un.org/development/desa/dpad/publication/un-desa-policy-brief-66-covid-19-and-the-least-developed-countries/.

44 Ibid.

45 Ibid.

46 "World's Most Vulnerable Countries Lack the Capacity to Respond to a Global Pandemic Credit: MFD/Elyas Alwazir | Office of the High Representative for the Least Developed Countries, Landlocked Developing Countries and Small Island Developing States," n.d., https://www.un.org/ohrlls/news/world%E2%80%99s-most-vulnerable-countries-lack-capacity-respond-global-pandemic-credit-mfdelyas-alwazir.

47 Wood, Daniel, "As Pandemic Deaths Add Up, Racial Disparities Persist — And in Some Cases Worsen," *NPR,* September 23, 2020, sec. Coronavirus By The Numbers, https://www.npr.org/sections/health-shots/2020/09/23/914427907/as-pandemic-deaths-add-up-racial-disparities-persist-and-in-some-cases-worsen.

48 "Community, Work, and School," Centers for Disease Control and Prevention, February 11, 2020, https://www.cdc.gov/coronavirus/2019-ncov/community/health-equity/race-ethnicity.html.

49 "Syrian Arab Republic: Recent Developments in Northwestern Syria Situation Report No. 24 - As of 26 January 2021 - Syrian Arab Republic," ReliefWeb, n.d., https://reliefweb.int/report/syrian-arab-republic/syrian-arab-republic-recent-developments-northwestern-syria-situation-14.

50 Yarar, Eralp, "Despair Replaces Hope, Risk of Coronavirus Outbreak Threatens Idlib," *Daily Sabah,* April 9, 2020, https://www.dailysabah.com/politics/news-analysis/despair-replaces-hope-risk-of-coronavirus-outbreak-threatens-idlib.

51 Alsayed, Ghaith, and Sarah El Deeb, "Virus Threat 'A New Terror' in Syria's Scarred Idlib Region," AP NEWS, April 20, 2021, https://apnews.com/article/ap-top-news-civil-wars-coronavirus-pandemic-syria-fa6f5a2f0c2f80922239ff96b98600e4.

52 Kanj, Sultan al-, "Humanitarian Disaster Looms over Syria's Idlib amid COVID-19

Surge - Al-Monitor: The Pulse of the Middle East," November 24, 2020, https://www.al-monitor.com/originals/2020/11/syria-idlib-hospitals-surge-coronavirus-cases.html.

53 "Doctors Expect 'Covid Catastrophe' in Syria," BBC News, October 27, 2020, https://www.bbc.com/news/av/world-middle-east-54697587.

54 Dean, Grace, "COVID-19 Vaccines Are Now Being Administered in the UK and US, but the Rollout May Take Years in Poorer Countries. Here Are the Major Challenges They Face," Business Insider, December 20, 2020, https://www.businessinsider.com/poor-countries-may-wait-years-covid-19-vaccines-2020-11.

55 Elliott, Larry, "The Coronavirus Crisis Has Brought the EU's Failings into Sharp Relief | Larry Elliott," *The Guardian*, March 29, 2020, http://www.theguardian.com/business/2020/mar/29/the-coronavirus-crisis-has-brought-the-eus-failings-into-sharp-relief.

56 Crowcroft, Orlando, "Coronavirus: 'Europe Is in a Fight for Its Life' Says von der Leyen," Euronews, March 26, 2020, https://www.euronews.com/2020/03/26/coronavirus-europe-is-in-a-fight-for-its-life-says-ursula-von-der-leyen.

57 "Turkey | Global Focus," December 20, 2019, https://reporting.unhcr.org/Turkey.

58 "204,000 Syrian Refugees Returned to Idlib since March, Turkey Records," *Daily Sabah*, July 19, 2020, https://www.dailysabah.com/politics/204000-syrian-refugees-returned-to-idlib-since-march-Turkey-records/news.

59 "Turkish Red Crescent Provides Tents for Idlib Refugees - Turkey News," *Hürriyet Daily News*, n.d., accessed August 9, 2021, https://www.hurriyetdailynews.com/turkish-red-crescent-provides-tents-for-idlib-refugees-152105.

60 Kazanci, Handan, "UN Envoy: Turkey's Refugee Response 'Exemplary,'" November 30, 2019, https://www.aa.com.tr/en/world/un-envoy-Turkeys-refugee-response-exemplary/1659784.

61 Ibid.

62 "Global Humanitarian Assistance Report 2019 - World," ReliefWeb, 2019, https://reliefweb.int/report/world/global-humanitarian-assistance-report-2019.

63 Ergocun, Gokhan, "Turkey Remains Most Generous Donor of Humanitarian Aid," Anadolu Agency, September 30, 2019, https://www.aa.com.tr/en/world/Turkey-remains-most-generous-donor-of-humanitarian-aid/1597587.

64 Habib, Mohshin, Christine Jubb, Salahuddin Ahmad, Masudur Rahman, and Henri Pallard, *Forced Migration of Rohingya: The Untold Experience*, Ottawa, Ontario: Ontario International Development Agency, Canada, 2018.

65 "Turkish President Erdoğan Remarks at United Nations General Assembly - General Debate | C-SPAN.Org," September 19, 2017, https://www.c-span.org/video/?434273-6/turkish-president-erdoan-remarks-united-nations-general-assembly-general-debate.

66 TİKA - Türk Birliği ve Koordinasyon Ajansı Başkanlığı, www.tika.gov.tr/tr/haber/turkiye_den_yemen'de_ic_savas_magdurlarina_gida_yardimi-57696.

67 "Turkish Development Assistance Reports - TİKA," 2019, https://www.tika.gov.tr/en/publication/list/turkish_development_assistance_reports-24.

68 "Turkey Keeps Breaking Records in Humanitarian Aid and Development Assistance - TİKA," n.d., https://www.tika.gov.tr/en/news/Turkey keeps_breaking_records_in_humanitarian_aid_and_development_assistance-49351.

69 "Turkish Development Assistance Reports - TİKA." 2019, p 18, https://www.tika.gov.tr/en/publication/list/turkish_development_assistance_reports-24.

70 "Türkiye Keeps Breaking Records in Humanitarian Aid and Development Assistance - TİKA."

71 Daily Sabah with Anadolu Agency, "Turkish Aid Agency TIKA Marks 28th Anniversary of Foundation," *Daily Sabah*, January 30, 2020. https://www.dailysabah.com/Turkey/2020/01/30/turkish-aid-agency-tika-marks-28th-anniversary-of-foundation.

72 Ibid.

73 "Türkiye Keeps Breaking Records in Humanitarian Aid and Development Assistance - TİKA."

74 "TIKA Continues to Be Lifeblood with Water Wells Drilled in Afghanistan - TİKA." n.d., accessed August 9, 2021, https://www.tika.gov.tr/en/news/tika_continues_to_be_lifeblood_with_water_wells_drilled_in_Afghanistan-19192.

75 Ibid.

76 "Türkiye Keeps Breaking Records in Humanitarian Aid and Development Assistance - TİKA."

77 "Cumhurbaşkanı Yardımcısı Oktay: Dünyadaki ülkelerin üçte ikisi Türkiye'den yardım talebinde bulundu," Anadolu Agency, May 15, 2020, retrieved June 4, 2020 from https://www.aa.com.tr/tr/koronavirus/cumhurbaskani-yardimcisi-oktay-dunyadaki-ulkelerin-ucte-ikisi-turkiyeden-yardim-talebinde-bulundu/1841441.

78 "Turkey Provides Medical Aid to 53 Countries to Tackle Coronavirus Pandemic," *Daily Sabah*, April 24, 2020, https://www.dailysabah.com/politics/Turkey-provides-medical-aid-to-53-countries-to-tackle-coronavirus-pandemic/news; Esen, Hasan, "UK Thanks Turkey for COVID-19 Support," December 4, 2020, https://www.aa.com.tr/en/europe/uk-thanks-Turkey-for-covid-19-support/1801433; *Daily Sabah* with Anadolu Agency, "Turkey Sends 2nd Batch of Medical Supplies to US amid Coronavirus Pandemic," April 30, 2020.

CHAPTER TWO

THE FAILURE OF INTERNATIONAL INSTITUTIONS

The international institutions that have defined the global system both during and after the Cold War are struggling to remain relevant in 21st-century geopolitics. In the aftermath of World War II, the U.S. government sponsored the reconstruction of Europe and built a liberal Western front against the Soviet bloc. But, with the end of the Cold War, the shortcomings and failures of these institutions were more openly exposed in a unipolar world. In the decade of the 1990s, institutions failed to respond to different global challenges, such as famine and ethnic cleansing, to prevent the emergence of civil wars, and to find a resolution for the enduring conflicts among different substate actors in newly emerging states in different parts of the world.

When the moment of unipolarity arrived with the collapse of the Soviet Union, the U.S. declared victory over the Soviets, but did not articulate a vision for the emerging global system. While some were quick to declare an ideological victory for the liberal capitalist system, many institutions that had been focused on meeting the communist threat could not adequately respond to the new era's challenges. In the absence of a clear, common threat for their members, these institutions found it difficult to redefine their common purpose. With an increasingly incoherent international system faced with a multitude of challenges, including threats such as international terrorism and genocide, international institutions remained heavily dependent on U.S. strategic priorities. The lack of interest and sensitivity among the European nations for the future of these international institutions, other than the European Union, and skepticism among non-Western major powers, such as Russia and China, toward these institutions also contributed to this utter failure.

During this period, the international institutions failed to take effective action to end civil wars and the reconstruction of countries that experienced years of war and conflict. Afghanistan was one of the most significant examples of these failures. Following the Soviet invasion, the international institutions did not take the necessary steps to reconcile the disputes, reconstruct the infrastructure, and restore the effective governance in the country. There was no meaningful action that could prevent Afghanistan from turning into a failed state in the midst of a geopolitically critical region for international security. The same failure presented itself during the conflicts in the Balkans. As the U.S. public, for instance, questioned the wisdom of becoming the "world's police officer," European powers lacked the wherewithal to confront a dramatic geopolitical transformation such as the dissolution of Yugoslavia, which resulted in acts of genocide. The most significant institutions of the international system, including the United Nations, the OSCE, and the EU, failed to stop the bloodshed and ethnic cleansing in the very heart of Europe. Particularly, the failure of the UN during this period resulted in critical skepticism of the international public about the role of international organizations.

A similar challenge presented itself as new threats emerged in international security. The challenge of international terrorism showed its ugly face soon after the fall of the Soviet Union, but the international community also remained largely reactive instead of working together to build a common defense framework to deal with terrorism. In President Erdoğan's words, "Neither the UN nor other international organizations have successfully defined international terrorism."[1] A common security architecture was not formed against international terrorism that would curb their operations, recruitment, and financing operations. Countries preferred to follow unilateral foreign policies in the absence of such a multilateral framework and mechanism.

Finally, when the COVID-19 outbreak started, existing international institutions failed to provide guidance and facilitate collective action against the worst pandemic in a century. As mentioned in the previous chapter, the World Health Organization was not effective in providing accurate and timely information to the international community about the pandemic. The statements by the organization generated a lot of controversy, and it lost public trust in a rather short period of time. Thus, in the post-Cold War world, the humanitarian, security, and health crises demonstrated that there are no effective and functional international institutions to handle these challenges. During the period after each crisis, the Turkish government asked for collective action by the international community to revise the missions and reform the management of the international institutions so that they can better prepare for the emerging challenges. However, most of the stakeholders in these institutions avoided taking on this responsibility and launching initiatives. The international institutions were seen either as an instrument of great power struggle or ineffective bureaucratic bodies. Only after the COVID-19 pandemic has the international community come to realize more openly that it is impossible to handle such an outbreak without active cooperation among states and coordination of national policies. While criticizing the failure of the international institutions, many started to realize that it would be extremely hard to resolve this crisis without an institutional framework.

United Nations: Under the Shadow of the Great Power Competition

The United Nations (UN) has been the most prominent institution of the post-World War II international system. The founding fathers designed this new institution to establish and maintain international peace and security, but it has failed to achieve this goal in many instances due largely to the imbalance in the power structure built into the UN system. As its membership grew over time, especially in the wake of the decolonization in Africa and the Asian subcontinent and later with the dissolution of the Soviet Union, the UN Security Council (UNSC) has continued to keep its original unequal distribution of power. The original five permanent members have kept their privileged position even after the end of the Cold War. Many debates and proposals to reform the UNSC have come to pass by leaders around the world, yet the nations with the veto power have refused to take meaningful collective action to ensure a more representative structure. This has meant that the national policies and strategies of permanent members have been prioritized over what has been agreed upon in a variety of conventions, agreements, and norms that define the international system. In turn, this has created a "deficit of legitimacy" due to the UNSC's "growing inability to find desperately needed solutions."[2]

As a result, the global issues of concern to most nations have not always been addressed by the UNSC. In most instances, only when such issues have been of direct concern to one or more of the permanent members, have we seen a serious mobilization on the part of the UNSC. The veto mechanism itself has served as the main vehicle through which human rights violations by oppressive regimes around the world have been tolerated and perpetuated. The veto power itself has given, in too many instances, the great powers license to block any meaningful action for maintaining peace around the world. The veto power has not only been used for national interests, but it has also been utilized as a bargaining chip in great power competition. Because of that, the most powerful organ of the most universal organization in the world has lost its credibility and legitimacy. Thus, today most people around the world do not expect a conflict or a security or humanitarian challenge to be resolved through the UN Security Council.

In addition to the unequal distribution of power, the key institutions of the organization also suffer from geographical imbalance. The balance of power represented at the UNSC implies a world dominated by the West counterbalanced, only to a limited extent, by China and Russia. It is a world where Africa has no representation and Asia is underrepresented by a large margin. There is no Latin American or Muslim country in the UN Security Council. The five privileged powers at the UNSC determine the destiny of the world in so many critical issues that the rest of the world appears powerless. Meanwhile the rest of the world has tried to band together in the past to compel the major powers to take certain actions for the benefit of humanity as a whole, but this has rarely succeeded. There are many examples of the failures of the UN as a direct result of the imbalance of the power structure that is the membership grouping of the UNSC itself; in this chapter we will discuss three major failures. These examples include the Israeli-Palestinian conflict, the Syrian civil war, and the COVID-19 pandemic, which underscore the international community's failure to provide peace and security as well as protect human rights.

The Israeli-Palestinian Conflict

The UN system's failure to ensure international peace and security could not be better exemplified than in the continuation of the Israeli-Palestinian conflict since 1947. Numerous UN resolutions have not only failed to bring an end to the conflict, but have also helped deepen the ongoing Israeli occupation of Palestinian lands. The political protection provided to Israel by the veto option of certain global powers has provided cover to an occupation that has destabilized the region while denying the rights of the Palestinian people. To be clear, often this has not been the consequence of disagreements and policy conflicts among the permanent members of the UNSC on how to resolve the conflict, but rather it is the consequence of the use of the veto power, mainly by the U.S., to perpetuate a power imbalance between the Israelis and the Palestinians. The special relationship built between the U.S. and Israel after 1967, and the power of the domestic lobbying groups in the U.S. in favor of Israel have made the American veto power a sure guarantee of protection from the reaction of the members of the UN.[3]

Israel has repeatedly benefited from the U.S. shielding it from international condemnation and criticism or any meaningful legal action against decades of illegal occupation and human rights violations. Between 1946 and 2002, the use of veto power occurred 252 times in the UN. Out of this number, the USSR/Russian Federation exercised its veto 121 times, most of which were used between 1946 and 1972 in the context of decolonization. The U.S. has exercised its veto power 76 times since 1972, more than any other permanent member of the UNSC. A total of 24 of these 76 instances were related to Palestine on various issues including conditions in the Occupied Territories, East Jerusalem, human rights violations, return of refugees, international monitoring initiatives, and the confiscation of Palestinian properties, among others.[4]

As a permanent member of the UNSC, the United States has used its veto power both as a threat and with actual votes to prevent Israel from being held responsible for various activities deemed illegal under international law. The U.S. commitment to Israel's security has manifested itself in the international arena as a form of diplomatic protection and immunity in the face of any criticism. The U.S. has threatened or used its veto to block any meaningful resolution that could have, at the very least, condemned Israel's continued illegal occupation and human rights violations. In February 2011, for instance, the U.S. vetoed a draft resolution that "would have characterized Israeli settlements in the West Bank and East Jerusalem as illegal" even though all permanent and non-permanent members of the UNSC were in favor.[5]

This veto came soon after President Obama won a historic election where he promised to refashion America's relations with the Islamic world. He was clearly constrained to move toward the fundamental change he advocated as a presidential candidate by domestic political considerations much to the dismay of Palestinians and the broader Arab world. The U.S. veto came in the wake of the beginning of the Arab Spring and although the resolution failed, American diplomacy was isolated in this instance.[6] Notwithstanding this diplomatic embarrassment, the U.S. was once again using its veto power at the UN to protect Israel from international condemnation at the expense of the Palestinians. The real problem has been that each veto the U.S. has used at the UN Security Council in regard to the Israeli-Palestinian dispute has been considered a green light by the Israeli government to continue its policies. The Israeli government presents the lack of a definitive UN position due to the deadlock at the UN Security Council as a source of legitimacy for the continuation of similar policies.

The latest instance of a resolution being vetoed by the U.S. occurred in June 2018. The resolution was adopted by the UN General Assembly, but opposed by the U.S. along with only seven other countries. The resolution stated that the UNSC "deplores the use of any excessive, disproportionate and indiscriminate force by the Israeli forces against Palestinian civilians in the Occupied Palestinian Territory, including East Jerusalem, and particularly in the Gaza Strip, including the use of live ammunition against civilian protestors, including children, as well as medical personnel and journalists, and expresses its grave concern at the loss of innocent lives."

Many countries around the world have interpreted the constant use of the veto power by the U.S. against the resolutions condemning Israel as a message to the world. This message says that indiscriminate violence imposed upon civilians is tolerated when perpetrated by a major ally of a world power. The aforementioned resolution, in fact, called on Israel to abide by the Fourth Geneva Convention, a bedrock of the post-World War II world order in terms of protection of civilians in times of war.[7] This could only be interpreted as a brazen disregard for international law and protection of human rights by the international community. Such actions prevent the emergence of collective action at the UN to resolve conflicts peacefully. A fair and sustainable solution to the problem necessitates a reformed UN Security Council and effective mechanisms within the organization to resolve the conflict.

The Syrian Civil War

The UN's failure to prevent human suffering and establish sustainable peace could not be starker than in the case of the Syrian civil war. A decade-old conflict has worsened over the years partly due to great power politics among the UNSC permanent members. Initially, major powers saw no serious national security interest in Syria and they refused to invest heavily in bringing about a political solution.

In this case, global competitors like Russia and China have consistently blocked any meaningful international action even in the form of condemnations or sanctions against the Syrian regime. As the U.S. refused to undertake any major diplomatic initiatives during the two terms of the Obama administration, Russia and China refused to cooperate in humanitarian actions that would have brought some relief to civilians in the war-torn country.

The UN General Assembly adopted its first resolution on Syria in December 2011. It condemned the "continued grave and systematic human rights violations by the Syrian authorities" and called upon the Assad regime to "implement the Plan of Action of the League of Arab States."[8] This resolution was intended to pave the way for a political solution, but it would prove to be ineffective because it lacked the backing of the UNSC. A draft resolution that had been presented to the UNSC two months earlier, in October 2011, which similarly condemned the "continued grave and systematic human rights violations and the use of force against civilians by the Syrian authorities," was vetoed by both Russia and China.[9] This first resolution formed the precedent whereby the General Assembly overwhelmingly votes to condemn and impose costs on the Syrian regime, but some UNSC members prevent any serious action against the regime.[10]

As Russia and China blocked diplomatic action, the Assad regime's persistent violations of human rights and the use of chemical weapons went unpunished as well. President Obama had drawn a "red line" on the use of chemical weapons by the Assad regime, but he shied away from enforcing it when it became undeniably clear the regime had, in fact, used chemical weapons. Russia offered a diplomatic lifeline to the U.S. administration in the form of an agreement to eliminate the weapons of mass destruction program that was part of the Assad regime. Already reluctant to enforce the red line, President Obama decided to take the offer as a "get out of jail free card" and help the regime survive since the agreement implicitly recognized the Assad regime as a legitimate governing entity.[11] In different instances throughout the civil war, Turkey and some other countries asked the UN and its bodies to play a more active role in order to alleviate the human suffering in the conflict and launch initiatives to find a political solution to the problem. Especially following the use of chemical weapons by the Assad regime, which was considered as the most critical and dangerous breach of international norms, large segments of the international community expected the UN to take meaningful action to prevent the repetition of the use of weapons of mass destruction. However, it was not achieved, and in later years, the Assad regime continued its chemical weapons attacks against civilians in Syria.

Due to the use of veto power and great power politics at the UNSC, as late as 2020, the UNSC was paralyzed on Syria to the degree that even humanitarian access to the country could not be guaranteed through international action.[12] Russia used its veto power on Syria-related matters 16 times,[13] and China supported most of these vetoes.[14] Given the increasing unwillingness of the other major actors to be more assertive, especially after 2013, the result has been catastrophic for Syria and the UN has failed to provide peace and stability or humanitarian protection in the conflict. As a result, the R2P principle could not be pursued by the international community in Syria.

The UNSC's inability to intervene meaningfully even in the form of a relatively simple and symbolic condemnation of chemical attacks shows the entrenched ineffectiveness and irrelevance of global governance.[15] The same body failed to protect "detainees and their families" persecuted by the Assad regime[16] and Syrian civilians, in general.[17] Furthermore, the great powers pursued resolutions at the UNSC that would enable their country's Syria policies instead of reducing violence and humanitarian suffering.[18] The UN High Commissioner for Human Rights criticized the use of the veto power by UNSC members to "block any unity of action, when it is needed the most" to protect the victims of the conflict.[19] Clearly, the overriding obstacle for the UN to change the course of the Syrian conflict, or at least to ease the humanitarian situation on the ground, has become the essential structure of the Security Council's decision-making process. Due to the veto power in the hands of the great powers, the General Assembly, as an international body with no real enforcement authority, can only contribute symbolically to peacemaking efforts. The national interests and the competition among the great powers have rendered the international community's response both ineffective and irrelevant at the expense of millions of civilians suffering from the consequences of conflicts across the world.

NATO: A Search for Purpose amidst Unprecedented Challenges

The North Atlantic Treaty Organization (NATO), established to provide security for Europe as the continent was being rebuilt following the end of World War II, connected the destinies of member states in a crucial way by considering an attack on one as an attack on all. NATO was intended to become the main organization for the transatlantic alliance to protect Europe against the Soviet Union. It served this function for decades and by all accounts it has been the most successful military alliance in modern history. After the fall of the Soviet Union in 1991, however, NATO's foundational raison d'etre along with its common enemy seemed to disappear. Surely, security threats and geopolitical challenges from Russia or other regions never actually ended. On the contrary, these challenges became even more complex and ubiquitous. Perhaps even more importantly, NATO should have been more prepared for a challenge like a pandemic as member states were threatened and weakened by the virus in an unprecedented manner. This was not a traditional threat yet it was a foreseeable one. In times like these, NATO should have been able to step up and mobilize a common response at the alliance level.

While NATO has been critical for the common defense of member states and has conducted successful military missions around the world, the increasing complexity of the changing geopolitical and geoeconomic dynamics have meant that NATO's strategic frameworks may not have kept pace with the changing times. Article 5 was invoked only once when the U.S. was attacked on September 11, 2001,[20] a decade after the disappearance of the Soviet military threat. The allies agreed on the common threat of global terrorism, but NATO was not necessarily able to augment a robust and all-encompassing counterterrorism framework. This is perhaps clearest when one looks at Türkiye's efforts in recent years to get NATO allies to agree on addressing the PKK/PYD/YPG terror threats coming out of northern Syria and northern Iraq.[21] As such, selective application of counterterrorism missions has undermined solidarity within NATO. In fact, as President Erdoğan puts it, "The most serious challenge the world faces ... is the hypocritical and insincere approach to terrorist organizations."[22] There has been a serious problem in terms of identification and definition of common challenges including a concept as central and critical as terrorism. The failure to reassure an alliance member like Türkiye on terrorism does not bode well for an organization that is supposed to serve as the main defense coordination mechanism among its members.

At the same time, we must acknowledge that NATO has made a conscious effort to address the shortcomings of its general strategic frameworks as well as emerging threats. It has also organized strategy groups for regional engagements covering the Mediterranean and the Middle East. While traditional NATO frameworks would emphasize external threats emanating from these countries and regions, some NATO alliance members have now forged relationships that could make common action very difficult. Their inability to create a template for common defense in a world more interrelated and connected than ever before has led to the questioning of NATO's viability. While no member state truly wants to abdicate the benefits of this alliance, many of them have questioned various of its aspects. Former U.S. president Trump's severe criticism of burden-sharing[23] and French President Macron's infamous "brain-dead"[24] description of the alliance reflect current dynamics. While some criticisms are perhaps unjustified, others arise from the fact that NATO has yet to achieve a comprehensive overhaul of its common defense strategy that addresses the real security concerns of its members given the present complex geopolitical circumstances. As a result of these challenges, NATO's record on providing much-needed leadership has been mixed on a variety of issues such as the refugee crisis, counterterrorism, and COVID-19.

The global migration crisis has grown to unsustainable levels over the past decade. The number of internally displaced persons, refugees, and asylum seekers around the world surpassed 80 million by the end of 2020.[25] Several NATO countries have been directly impacted from the flow of refugees due to war and instability in the Middle East and North Africa. Türkiye has shouldered the lion's share among NATO allies by hosting close to 5 million refugees while Germany has hosted more than a million refugees. In this crisis, NATO has failed to create a comprehensive plan of action to deal with this unprecedented crisis while European partners have tried to keep refugees out through negotiations with Türkiye. Seeing refugees as a potential security threat, EU leaders and many U.S. politicians have tried to appease their self-interested concerns with humanitarian aid instead of crafting plans to absorb more refugees. The political implications of this crisis have been serious as it arguably became a major driver for the UK's departure from the European Union,[26] not to mention rising xenophobia and Islamophobia throughout Europe. Türkiye's NATO allies had different national policies regarding the migration crisis, which was largely focused on security instead of humanitarianism. Neither the EU nor NATO was able to create a comprehensive strategy that addressed the security and humanitarian aspects of the crisis.

Many EU countries failed to implement a humanitarian approach when faced with large numbers of refugees at their borders, and suffered from the persistent structural problems of their national and Europe-wide asylum systems.[27] Some NATO members even faced calls from the UN Refugee Agency (UNHCR) to abide by the principles of the Common European Asylum System, but failed to extend protection to refugees.[28] While NATO has often been mobilized to provide humanitarian aid to disaster-stricken regions around the world in the past,[29] the ongoing migration crisis with broad security and political implications presented a different kind of challenge for the organization. NATO allies focused on relieving the burden on countries like Greece and Italy, while many European members chose either to restrict movement or close their borders to asylum seekers. This was clearly a challenge that required a NATO-wide strategy to limit its impact.

NATO allies not only failed to help create a supranational migration strategy or a much-needed "global compact on refugees" as advocated by the UN,[30] but they also failed to protect the borders of member nations like Türkiye. During the Libya intervention, NATO allies applied the R2P principle in the name of protecting civilians, but when a much more dire situation occurred in Syria, intervention never came. Granted that the situation in Syria was different with actors having a much more obstructionist role, NATO should have pushed harder to end the Syrian conflict in order to prevent the humanitarian catastrophe in the making. Türkiye, a NATO ally, was directly threatened by developments in Syria and the movement of millions of displaced persons destabilized the Middle East and Europe. Türkiye tried to bring a menu of options (including a safe zone, a buffer zone, and a no-fly zone) to NATO and called for intervention in Syria[31] but to no avail. NATO solidarity should have mobilized allies to intervene to protect NATO's credibility as well as the stability of its member states.

One can certainly not expect NATO to solve every problem, but a challenge of such magnitude as the refugee crisis has had far-reaching consequences for NATO allies. Regional instability, border security, human trafficking, humanitarian challenges, and intra-NATO disagreements have become persistent problems arising from the refugee crisis. Some NATO allies could have shouldered the lion's share of the burden as a gesture of strengthening the alliance's unity and solidarity. The destabilizing effect of the crisis on the allies has been undeniable. Containing the crisis and demonstrating unwavering support for the most affected allies like Türkiye should have been the absolute minimum response by the alliance. The failures on this front have not only undermined the cause of the NATO alliance, but have also weakened the resolve for common defense. NATO can and should do more to develop a common humanitarian and security response to this lingering challenge. This is particularly important since so many international organizations have failed to contain and remedy the adverse consequences of this crisis.

NATO's approach to terrorism fundamentally changed following the September 11 terror attacks in the United States. As the U.S. invoked Article 5, the first and only time in the history of the alliance, the conception of defense against global terrorism has dramatically changed. As a NATO ally was attacked by an al-Qaeda terrorist group based in Afghanistan, the member states acknowledged the unique nature of the encompassing circumstances. NATO would respond to this threat by engaging far away from its traditional geographic reach. The emergence of transnational terrorism meant that NATO allies could no longer be contented merely with protecting their national borders. Furthermore, the complex set of threats emanating from rogue actors and nations included the proliferation of weapons of mass destruction as well. The sense of an emergence of a new age of global terrorism and the spread of weapons of mass destruction shaped the evolution of security concepts. Thus, NATO took on new missions as required by this new age of more complex, intertwined, and non-traditional threats.

Even though the U.S. declared a global war on terror and set out to invade Afghanistan and then Iraq, many NATO allies had misgivings about the Iraq war and opposed it. There was clearly a disconnect between the war on terror and what it should entail in terms of its execution. This was not simply the result of the U.S. administration adopting a "with us or against us framework." It was clearly a result of the failure within NATO to define the threat, measure capabilities and potential contributions of ally nations, examine willingness to contribute, and allocate resources accordingly. This created a serious mismatch between the newly defined counterterrorism goals and how NATO missions were to be conducted. This incongruity was most obvious when al-Qaeda conducted an attack in Madrid in March 2004, and NATO did not discuss anything related to collective defense in this instance.[32] The NATO Response Force (NRF) was conceived as a force for "swift crisis deployment," but the structural problems built into the NATO structure (i.e., members' veto power over when and how to use it) and its small size at 21,000 troops[33] meant this force could not undertake a challenge such as the global war on terror except to assist it in a supportive capacity. The larger problem, of course, remains the fact that defining a common threat even in the case of something as real and concrete as terrorism has become more elusive.

NATO allies have not been able to come to a common understanding on the fundamental parameters that define terrorism and how it should be countered internationally. One difficulty with the emerging counterterrorism framework, for example, had to do with "state sponsors" of terrorism, where not all NATO allies agreed on which countries fit this definition. In Istanbul, in 2004, NATO allies committed to a "multi-faceted and comprehensive" counterterrorism strategy and agreed that NATO forces would seek to "deter, disrupt, defend and protect against terrorist attacks, or threat of attacks ... including by acting against these terrorists and those who harbor them." But, when it came to identifying countries to be targeted, the issue turned out to be much more complicated.[34] As a result, some have argued that NATO should stay out of the business of counterterrorism, which would probably mean confining the organization to its historical roots in terms of Europe's defense. As such, both the lack of political consensus in defining global terror activities and how to deal with them, and Europe's inability to adjust its foreign policy made it ever more difficult for NATO to become an effective force in counterterrorism.

Arriving at a common definition of terrorism and other threats in the age of "hybrid threats" has frustrated and eluded NATO allies. NATO's Strategic Concept, accepted by the members in Lisbon in 2010, reconfirmed the commitment to "deter and defend against any threat of aggression, and against emerging security challenges where they threaten the fundamental security of individual Allies or the Alliance as a whole." Most transnational security challenges faced by the allied nations consist of numerous threats posed by a combination of various sources, including organized crime, arms trafficking, human smuggling, terrorism as well as political violence, among others. The hybrid nature of these threats is often not fully addressed by NATO and member states face a multitude of them consistently. For instance, Türkiye has struggled against PKK terrorism, which has involved the intimidation and killing of civilians, arms smuggling, human and drug trafficking, political violence, and international terrorism. Another NATO member, namely the U.S., however, defines the Syrian branch of this terror group (YPG) as a separate organization that deserves to be armed to fight against another terror group, DAESH. What is more astonishing is that the U.S. government officials and institutions have acknowledged the ties and congruity between the PKK and the YPG, even admitting that there is no real separation between the two entities.

This is one clear example of the failure of NATO to define and identify in distinct terms the basic parameters of terroristic activities and what to do about them. The resulting damage to the coherence of the NATO alliance is a real handicap. Türkiye is a major contributor to NATO and to the security of its allies, thanks to its large army, its 2% defense budget spending, and major contributions to NATO missions around the world. Türkiye cooperates with allies on transnational threats from piracy to terrorism and many areas on the spectrum of concern. Türkiye has raised relevant questions about the lack of support and commitment to Turkish security by NATO allies who have undermined Türkiye's security by supporting the YPG/PKK terror organization. Thus, the issue of the PKK is becoming a major source of contention for NATO while the PKK's increasingly sophisticated terrorist propaganda cannot be confronted satisfactorily. NATO is failing to articulate a functioning definition of terrorism, but instead has relied upon double standards based on the political preferences of member countries. Türkiye finds itself without sincere support and empathy on this issue from its closest allies within NATO.

NATO must create a new counterterrorism framework that addresses the lack of common action and common definitions when it comes to existing and emerging terrorism threats. The increasingly sophisticated disinformation and propaganda tools employed by these groups should not be allowed to cloud the judgment of an organization like NATO. Left unaddressed, the result will be a chaotic situation where the "greatest military alliance in history" cannot come to a common definition and understanding of terrorism. The alliance members must take each other's concerns seriously if effective cooperation in the service of regional stability and peace is to be achieved. The most recent agreement to create a "NATO 2030" vision framework promises to tackle an ambitious and broadened agenda beyond the traditional security issues. The member states have shown that they understand and appreciate the much more complex set of issues awaiting them in the future. However, this broadened agenda might likely create further divisions and disagreements as individual states' priorities differ over a variety of common challenges. NATO has positioned itself to confront a broader agenda in the rest of this decade, but achieving institutional effectiveness will almost certainly remain a major challenge in the years ahead.

Global Health Crisis

The failure to prevent the early spread of the coronavirus pandemic represented a grave failure of the international community with long-term consequences, which have yet to be properly assessed. The most powerful nations showed an immediate reflex of self-preservation and erected barriers to protect themselves against the virus instead of charting a course of international cooperation from the very beginning. The lack of global leadership on a challenge that was sure to threaten the health of humanity has been fatally consequential. The richest nations not only failed to lead the world in creating a collective response, but they reverted to an "our country first" approach by restricting travel and circulation of people as well as goods and services. Smart implementation of reasonable restrictions on human travel should have been welcome and Türkiye pursued such a policy. However, many nations imposed export restrictions on personal protective equipment as well as medical workers and experts, rendering international cooperation impossible.

The international institutions whose job it was to warn the world and provide reliable and accurate guidance on epidemics failed to function properly. The World Health Organization (WHO) was charged with the task of coordinating the response in times of global pandemics such as COVID-19. It was also this international body that was tasked with facilitating data sharing and pooling of expertise among nations on infectious diseases. The organization did not simply fail to coordinate the initial global response and information-sharing, but, in fact, became one of the main reasons for the failure to provide guidance rapidly because of its inadequate, ambiguous, and conflicting messaging on the pandemic origins. This was yet another example of the failures of global health governance where national policies were prioritized over the interests of the global community at large.

It is important to remember that the WHO as an organization has also been under the pressure of different countries and governments. When the WHO declared a global public health emergency on January 30, 2020, COVID-19 had already spread to at least three continents. While the WHO warned nations to be prepared in early February, it also urged nations not to close their borders based on fears that nations might hide the information about the extent of the outbreaks. But the WHO also lacked authority to investigate or demand information from the nations that fund it.[35] It is a flawed organizational structure, in the sense that it relies on the good-faith efforts of member nations. In 2021, questions had yet to be answered as there was widespread evidence that the true extent of the outbreak and the airborne nature of the disease were not shared transparently with the rest of the world. Lacking an authority to compel the gathering of such critical information, the WHO's efforts proved to be too slow to keep up with the spread of the disease.

The WHO was not only slow in declaring a public health emergency but also too cautiously diplomatic as it relied on the information provided by member countries about the way in which the transmission of the virus occurred. The WHO was informed of "cases of pneumonia of unknown etiology ... detected in Wuhan City" on December 31, 2019.[36] On January 14, 2020, the WHO's Twitter account stated, "The Chinese authorities have found no clear evidence of human-to-human transmission of the novel coronavirus."[37] It was only on January 22, 2020 that the WHO confirmed that the virus was transmitted between humans. The WHO and China established a joint mission and prepared a report in mid-February,[38] but it was not until March 11, 2020 that the WHO declared the outbreak a pandemic.[39] The speed of data collection, the dissemination of information about the disease, the delays in conducting a mission, and an overreliance on the data provided by a member country all contributed to the loss of precious time in the initial stages of the pandemic. The organization, as the world discovered, was structurally vulnerable to lack of transparency, misinformation, and political influence.[40]

These developments demonstrated that the WHO not only failed to take rapid action to warn nations about the severity of the crisis, but also failed to enable world leaders to coordinate a quick global response. Even worse, the institution became embroiled in political controversy with a blame game among the great powers. As a result, the Trump administration threatened to pull U.S. funding from the WHO largely due to the administration's aversion to multilateral organizations but also because of its own lack of preparation for the pandemic.[41] In the early days of the pandemic, when the nature of the virus and the extent of its spread were yet to be determined, many nations struggled to respond effectively. The lack of information and transparency as well as the failures of the WHO complicated responses, as countries hesitated on how to handle the uncertainty of the circumstances. To slow the spread of the virus and prevent mass deaths, many countries implemented complete or partial shutdowns that practically devastated many economies. For instance in NATO, instead of focusing on coordination and cooperation in the rapid deployment of medical assistance to those affected the most, many alliance members implemented bans on export of medical equipment and imposed travel restrictions.[42] This affected countries where the early outbreak of the coronavirus was most severe and as a result they could not receive urgently needed help in a timely manner. Many NATO member states lacked national-scale capacity and resources, as they had already been relying on manufacturing activities in Asia. Restrictions on medical resources and travel made it more difficult for them to secure the most basic personal protective equipment (PPE) for their health professionals, even many months after the start of the pandemic.[43]

Italy, for instance, was hit very hard early on, and Italians found themselves unprepared, overwhelmed, and helpless. As NATO's response was not well coordinated at the political level, it remained largely a logistical operation and even NATO member citizens such as Italians were dismayed by the lack of assistance by their transatlantic partners. China capitalized on "humanitarian diplomacy" by sending help to Italy.[44] Türkiye made a conscientious effort to help NATO allies[45] and dozens of other countries around the world, which NATO praised.[46] But, overall coordination and solidarity remained well below expectations. NATO was effective in delivering emergency help and rapid response, but the organization did not function as a platform to enable a political response by the allies and other countries took advantage of this alliance failure in the face of the most serious global challenge of our time.

In discussions about forthcoming challenges facing NATO, there is a wide array of traditional as well as novel issues. NATO has done a lot in terms of trying to anticipate and respond to threats in a variety of non-traditional realms including cybersecurity. Although pandemics were on the list of NATO's potential challenges, it became clear that the full extent of political, health, and budgetary concerns could not be fully foreseen when an airborne virus became a reality. None of these potential and actual threats will disappear anytime soon, and NATO will have to be prepared for a much more complex security environment[47] in an era where national defense budgets are under ever-growing pressure.[48] As countries will need to make difficult choices in terms of burden-sharing, they know they cannot easily compromise on matters of common defense. Yet, the shortcomings and disappointments among some alliance members will need to be remedied. Otherwise, NATO may end up being irrelevant in the face of a new generation of economic, technological, and political shifts.

The international organization that should have provided a sense of political unity and common purpose in the face of such a global challenge is the United Nations. However, the UN was not very effective in its response to the pandemic. The UNSC, for example, was virtually devoid of any serious discussions or resolutions focused on fashioning a global road map in dealing with the political, social, and economic impact of the pandemic. The UN launched a $2 billion "global humanitarian response" plan to fight the impact of the pandemic in the poorest nations, beginning in late March 2020, but its focus needs to be broadened. As the UN lacked necessary funding mechanisms for such a global challenge, Secretary General Antonio Guterres appealed to G-20 nations for funding to suppress the virus, ban tariffs, facilitate cross-border trade, and enable transportation of medical equipment. Guterres also called for "the urgent launch of a large-scale, coordinated stimulus package in the trillions of dollars" to help businesses, workers, and households in those countries.[49] These calls did not generate a robust global response as many nations focused on their own economies and national priorities.

Faced with the biggest challenge and the most severe threat to human security in recent memory, international organizations such as the WHO, NATO, and the UN have not performed efficiently, at best. Once again, we have been witnessing a situation where the international organizations (even those whose job it is to lead in a time like this) have lacked the capacity to respond quickly and overcome politics to provide global leadership for humanity. From day one, the most powerful nations should have come together and agreed on a path that would provide clear guidelines and dynamic responses to such a deadly virus. Many nations simply forgot about international collaboration and the common fate of humanity in the absence of such leadership. Türkiye repeatedly called for international solidarity and a global response by sending aid to many nations around the world, limiting travel and the movement of goods and services based only on real data, and putting forward several proposals in the international forums for cooperation. The impact of these efforts was limited by the rich nations' self-centered national policies and the failures of international organizations that are responsible for leading in such trying times. The pandemic has shown, yet again, that the only way to address the global common challenges is for the international system to undergo an honest and thorough reform process prioritizing the security and safety of all humanity and not only the citizens of the most powerful nations.

Türkiye's Reform Proposals

Türkiye has long advocated for reforming international institutions by joining some other nations who have also called for the UN to be reformed. Certainly, this is a dialogue that needs to continue and the UNSC's inclusion should be broadened to other nation-states. One obvious reason for delaying this dialogue is that the current permanent members are privileged and given enormous power by the weight of their veto, which they are unwilling to dilute. There is also no clear mechanism or set of standards established to admit new members based on either population size, economic power, or performance on certain metrics. Türkiye has proposed that the UNSC membership should be open to others based on a set of dynamic criteria decided upon by the UN General Assembly. The permanent seats should be increased to, perhaps, 20 and the membership should be open to the "rest." To distinguish this from the G-20, where the top economies of the world congregate, UNSC membership should involve a comprehensive set of standards that would give a chance to the least developed countries to enter the UNSC. Including the top 20 most powerful nations in the UNSC would defeat the purpose of reform and would do little more than enlarge the pool of the privileged without addressing the underlying gaps that cause global inequality.

In addition to changing the size and the eligibility criteria for the UNSC, Türkiye has advocated for addressing the plight of underdeveloped nations. In the hyperconnected world of the 21st century, no challenge stays where it is. As clearly shown by the pandemic, humanity is vulnerable to sudden global disruption from infectious diseases, natural disasters, and cyber vulnerabilities, just to name a few. In the face of such global threats with such disruptive potential, nations have no choice but to pool their efforts to collaborate on a rapid response. Many nations, which are often forgotten or left behind in such times of crisis, are active geopolitical participants in the global community and to neglect them would cause peril that eventually engulfs all nations. Türkiye has risen to be a representative voice for such nations at international forums and will continue to do so. But, Türkiye's own voice, along with those of other nation-states it has sought to include, should be heard at the UN and by NATO through institutional structural reform. Both the UN and NATO are structured in a way that global challenges only matter when they threaten the West directly. This is not only unfair, but also unwise for the sake of the West itself. Türkiye is active in Africa and Asia by advocating for peace and stability in countries such as Somalia and assuring the rights of the Rohingya Muslims in Myanmar. Ankara understands that collectively the human community cannot be safe and cannot prosper if the least developed parts of the world are unstable and perpetually in crisis.

At the same time, Türkiye has advocated for an international response in the Syrian civil war and the unprecedented refugee crisis it created in the region. Türkiye has participated in several multinational operations conducted by NATO, including the mission in Afghanistan. Türkiye argues for international intervention when it serves the purpose of regional stability and peace, but not when it is in the interest of a few countries. The current UNSC and NATO structures discussed above create a situation where interventions are carried out unilaterally by the great powers and they are not done for the purposes of securing stability and peace. The R2P principle, for instance, has created too much friction in the international community because it was not conceptualized with input by a broader spectrum of nations who could have strengthened the objective of finding consensus on the principle. One reform idea that Türkiye has proposed would establish clear standards for international intervention and a sanctions regime to be imposed in cases of civil wars such as in Syria. With a clear set of criteria for intervention, established and voted on by the UN General Assembly, the international community could play a constructive role that would have both legitimacy and deterrence against repressive and violent regimes like the Assad regime.

These reform proposals by Türkiye could remedy some main structural problems and lack of action by the international community regarding ongoing major conflicts around the world. The international aid system, for example, suffers from the fact that most of the funds remain in the West in the form of administrative costs, profits for the humanitarian aid companies, or job creation for certain sectors. Peacekeeping operations are often aligned with the interests of large powers. Access to vaccines, for instance, is prioritized for the privileged few while the poorer nations are left behind. NATO's regional dialogues have been less than effective in addressing the migrant crisis in the Mediterranean, for instance. Türkiye's reform proposals emphasize considerations of inclusiveness, diversity, and justice. The world can no longer afford not to address the lack of attention on global imbalances, as reflected in the very structure of the institutions that have served as the backbone of the international system. Türkiye's proposals to "right-size" the heavy imbalance built into the international organizations should be taken more seriously in order to create a more stable environment that considers larger issues such as the refugee crisis and, in the longer term, climate change.

There is no question that the future holds formidable challenges. The most critical institutions of the Western alliance discussed in this chapter, such as the WHO, the UN, and NATO, have struggled to address 21st-century challenges and adapt accordingly, although there has been some success in certain areas. On many global issues, their response has either been entangled in great power politics or has fallen prey to lack of strategic foresight. One should expect that the institutional legacy of the Cold War will continue to proceed for some time to come. But the world continues to change at a seemingly accelerated pace and if these international bodies cannot adapt and lead, they will become so irrelevant and impotent that they will cease to function in any effective capacity. More importantly, underlying global issues and crises will become more prominent and their effects will be aggravated.

The window of opportunity for reforming, rehabilitating, and repurposing international institutions is active. The daily events indicate major shifts in power dynamics and technological changes happening at a quickening pace on a continuous basis. These changes require continuous routine adjustment and adaptation to evolving conditions for all actors - both governmental and civilian. The cost of being left behind is too high to ignore, particularly as nations are forever in competitive mode. Nevertheless, it is only through cooperation and collaboration with the guidance of long-term views that one can make sense of short-term challenges and handle crises cogently and coherently. Multilateral cooperation among nations should and can occur with an unprecedented breadth and depth of scope and scale. At the same time, one must be vigilantly cognizant of the fact that national identity continues to be a bedrock of importance that must be accounted for and sensitized in action and response. These dual challenges are not necessarily insurmountable, if indeed international institutions accept inclusion, diversity, equity, and accessibility as essential traits underlying how they articulate their objectives.

ENDNOTES

1 Erdoğan, Recep Tayyip, *A Fairer World Is Possible: A Proposed Model for United Nations Reform*, Istanbul, September 2021, p. 44.

2 Ibid., p. 63.

3 Mearsheimer, John J, *The Israel Lobby and U.S. Foreign Policy*, 1st edition, New York: FSG Adult, 2008.

4 Sarsar, Saliba, "The Question of Palestine and United States Behavior at the United Nations," *International Journal of Politics, Culture, and Society* 17 (3): 457-70, 2004, https://doi.org/10.1023/B:IJPS.0000019613.01593.5e.

5 "Israel: Background and U.S. Relations," n.d., accessed August 9, 2021, https://www.everycrsreport.com/reports/RL33476.html. 58.

6 Usher, Graham, "Letter from the UN: After the U.S. Veto on Settlements," *Journal of Palestine Studies* 40 (3): 74–83, 2011, https://doi.org/10.1525/jps.2011.xl.3.74.

7 Ibid.

8 "Security Council Unanimously Adopts Resolution 2254 (2015), Endorsing Road Map for Peace Process in Syria, Setting Timetable for Talks | Meetings Coverage and Press Releases," n.d., https://www.un.org/press/en/2015/sc12171.doc.htm.

9 "Russia and China Veto Draft Security Council Resolution on Syria," UN News, October 4, 2011, https://news.un.org/en/story/2011/10/390412-russia-and-china-veto-draft-security-council-resolution-syria.

10 "Kofi Annan's Six-Point Plan," Aljazeera, March 27, 2012, https://www.aljazeera.com/news/2012/3/27/kofi-annans-six-point-plan-for-syria.

11 Hill, Fiona, "Putin Scores on Syria," September 11, 2013, https://www.foreignaffairs.com/articles/russian-federation/2013-09-11/putin-scores-syria.

12 "Humanitarian Aid to Syrians Threatened as Russia and China Veto Proposals at U.N," *Washington Post*, n.d., accessed August 9, 2021, https://www.washingtonpost.com/national-security/humanitarian-aid-to-syrians-threatened-as-russia-and-china-veto-proposals-at-un/2020/07/10/96c87a0c-c2d4-11ea-b178-bb7b05b94af1_story.html.

13 "Syria," 2021, Global Centre for the Responsibility to Protect, May 31, 2021, https://www.globalr2p.org/countries/syria/.

14 "Russia, China Veto Syria Aid via Turkey for Second Time This Week," Reuters, July 10, 2020, sec. China, https://www.reuters.com/article/us-syria-security-un-idUSKBN24B2NW.

15 Nadin, Peter, "How the UN Security Council Failed Syria," August 30, 2017. https://www.lowyinstitute.org/the-interpreter/how-un-security-council-failed-syria.

16 "UN Security Council 'Utterly Failed' Syrian Detainees; A Victim Voices Her Plea to 'End Impunity and Stop This Horror,'" UN News, August 7, 2019, https://news.un.org/en/story/2019/08/1043891.

17 "Security Council Backsliding on Duty to Protect Syria's Civilians, Rights Advocate Stresses, amid Calls to Protect Hospitals, Review Deconfliction Accords | Meetings Coverage and Press Releases," n.d., accessed August 10, 2021, https://www.un.org/press/en/2019/sc13903.doc.htm.

18 "Dueling U.N. Resolutions on Syria Both Fail, Leaving Millions at Risk," *Washington Post.*, n.d., https://www.washingtonpost.com/national-security/dueling-un-resolutions-on-syria-both-fail-leaving-millions-at-risk/2019/09/19/3d9e71b4-db2d-11e9-a688-303693fb4b0b_story.html.

19 "OHCHR | 37th Session of the Human Rights Council," n.d., accessed August 10, 2021, https://www.ohchr.org/EN/NewsEvents/Pages/DisplayNews.aspx?NewsID=22702&LangID=E.

20 "Collective Defence - Article 5," NATO, n.d., accessed August 10, 2021. http://www.nato.int/cps/en/natohq/topics_110496.htm.

21 Çelik, Mehmet, "Türkiye Faults NATO for Inactivity against US-Backed Terror Army on Syrian Border," *Daily Sabah*, January 17, 2018, https://www.dailysabah.com/diplomacy/2018/01/17/Turkey-faults-nato-for-inactivity-against-us-backed-terror-army-on-syrian-border.

22 Erdoğan, *A Fairer World Is Possible*, p. 85.

23 Davis, Julie Hirschfeld, "Trump Warns NATO Allies to Spend More on Defense, or Else," *The New York Times*, July 2, 2018, sec. World, https://www.nytimes.com/2018/07/02/world/europe/trump-nato.html.

24 "Nato Alliance Experiencing Brain Death, Says Macron," BBC News, November 7, 2019, sec. Europe, https://www.bbc.com/news/world-europe-50335257.

25 "Figures at a Glance," UNHCR, June 18, 2020. https://www.unhcr.org/figures-at-a-glance.html.

26 Caporaso, James A, "Europe's Triple Crisis and the Uneven Role of Institutions: The Euro, Refugees and Brexit," *JCMS: Journal of Common Market Studies* 56 (6): 1345–61, 2018, https://doi.org/10.1111/jcms.12746.

27 H Beirens, Hanne, "Cracked Foundation, Uncertain Future: Structural Weaknesses in the Common European Asylum System," Migrationpolicy.Org, March 16, 2018, https://www.migrationpolicy.org/research/structural-weaknesses-common-european-asylum-system.

28 Wilkes, Sybella, "Syria Crisis: UNHCR Urges European Union States to Honour Their Asylum System Principles," UNHCR, n.d., accessed August 10, 2021. https://www.unhcr.org/news/latest/2012/10/507d4c586/syria-crisis-unhcr-urges-european-union-states-honour-asylum-system-principles.html.

29 "NATO-UNHCR Airlift Extended as Aid Is Rushed to Pakistan before the Winter," UNHCR, n.d., accessed August 10, 2021. https://www.unhcr.org/news/press/2005/11/436a3cf14/nato-unhcr-airlift-extended-aid-rushed-pakistan-winter.html.

30 Türk, Volker, and Madeline Garlick, "From Burdens and Responsibilities to Opportunities: The Comprehensive Refugee Response Framework and a Global Compact on Refugees," *International Journal of Refugee Law* 28 (4): 656-78, 2016. https://doi.org/10.1093/ijrl/eew043.

31 Rettman, Andrew, "Turkey Calls Emergency Nato Talks on Syria," EUobserver, June 25, 2012, https://euobserver.com/foreign/116743.

32 Kay, Sean, "What Went Wrong with NATO?" *Cambridge Review of International Affairs* 18 (1): 69–83, 2005, https://doi.org/10.1080/09557570500059589.

33 Ibid., 76.

34 Brown, David, "'The War on Terrorism Would Not Be Possible without NATO': A Critique," *Contemporary Security Policy* 25 (3): 409-29, 2004, https://doi.org/10.1080/1352326042000330583.

35 McKay, Betsy and Drew Hinshaw, "How Coronavirus Overpowered the World Health Organization," *The Wall Street Journal*, August 28, 2020, sec. US, https://www.wsj.com/articles/the-who-was-built-to-guard-global-health-it-was-too-weak-for-coronavirus-11598625537.

36 "Pneumonia of Unknown Cause – China," January 5, 2020, https://www.who.int/emergencies/disease-outbreak-news/item/2020-DON229.

37 World Health Organization (WHO), "Preliminary Investigations Conducted by the Chinese Authorities Have Found No Clear Evidence of Human-to-Human Transmission of the Novel #coronavirus (2019-NCoV) Identified in #Wuhan, #China. Https://T.Co/Fnl5P877VG," Twitter, January 14, 2020, https://twitter.com/WHO/status/1217043229427761152.

38 "Report of the WHO-China Joint Mission on Coronavirus Disease 2019 (COVID-19)," n.d., https://www.who.int/publications-detail-redirect/report-of-the-who-china-joint-mission-on-coronavirus-disease-2019-(covid-19).

39 "Timeline: WHO's COVID-19 Response," n.d., https://www.who.int/emergencies/diseases/novel-coronavirus-2019/interactive-timeline.

40 Gilsinan, Kathy, "How China Deceived the WHO," The Atlantic, April 12, 2020, https://www.theatlantic.com/politics/archive/2020/04/world-health-organization-blame-pandemic-coronavirus/609820/.

41 Tufekci, Zeynep, "The WHO Shouldn't Be a Plaything for Great Powers," The Atlantic, April 16, 2020, https://www.theatlantic.com/health/archive/2020/04/why-world-health-organization-failed/610063/.

42 Boykoff, Pamela, Clare Sebastian, and Valentina Di Donato, "In the Race to Secure Medical Supplies, Countries Ban or Restrict Exports," CNN, n.d., https://www.cnn.com/2020/03/27/business/medical-supplies-export-ban/index.html.

43 Cohen, Dan, "Op-Ed: Why a PPE Shortage Still Plagues America and What We Need to Do about It," CNBC, August 22, 2020, https://www.cnbc.com/2020/08/22/coronavirus-why-a-ppe-shortage-still-plagues-the-us.html.

44 Cui, Mu, "COVID-19: China Steps in to Help Italy Battle the Virus | DW | 24.03.2020," DW.COM., March 24, 2020, https://www.dw.com/en/covid-19-china-steps-in-to-help-italy-battle-the-virus/a-52901560.

45 "Coronavirus Response: Turkish Medical Aid Arrives in Spain and Italy," NATO, n.d., http://www.nato.int/cps/en/natohq/news_174826.htm.

46 Daily Sabah with Anadolu Agency, "NATO Chief Praises Turkey's Efforts for Solidarity amid Coronavirus Pandemic," *Daily Sabah*, April 15, 2020, https://www.dailysabah.com/politics/diplomacy/nato-chief-praises-Turkeys-efforts-for-solidarity-amid-coronavirus-pandemic.

47 Tardy, Thierry, "COVID-19: Shaping Future Threats and Security Policies," COVID-19: NATO Defense College, 2020, https://www.jstor.org/stable/resrep25148.8.

48 Babst, Stefanie, "The Coronavirus Pandemic Hits NATO: Five Potential Implications," April 14, 2020, https://www.europeanleadershipnetwork.org/commentary/the-coronavirus-pandemic-hits-nato-five-potential-implications/.

49 "Funding the Fight against COVID-19 in the World's Poorest Countries," United Nations, n.d., https://www.un.org/en/un-coronavirus-communications-team/funding-fight-against-covid-19-world%E2%80%99s-poorest-countries.

CHAPTER THREE

PERSISTENT CONFLICTS AROUND THE WORLD

The long list of protracted conflicts around the world today attests to the unfortunate and ongoing failure of the international community to provide adequate and competent conflict resolution mechanisms. Every international institution, which was originally founded to support international cooperation and solidarity, repeatedly fails in addressing the impact of long-running conflicts in various regions across the globe. Outright invasions in places like Afghanistan and Iraq; civil and proxy wars in Syria, Yemen, and Somalia; deepening occupations and human rights violations in Palestine; frozen conflicts in Cyprus; military annexations in Ukraine and Crimea; and regional proxy wars such as that between the Gulf, Iran, and Israel are only some of the examples that indicate the ongoing failure of the international conflict resolution efforts. This failure emanates from the structural imbalances built into the international organizations rather than simply a lack of effort on the part of the international community - though that is a big factor as well. When a conflict occurs somewhere in the world, the big powers immediately prioritize their national interests and then attempt to shape outcomes according to those interests rather than what peace and stability might require. What ends up happening most often in these conflict zones is a clash of national and international interests rather than a unity of purpose on the part of the international community to achieve a peaceful outcome for the sake of the international system. The result is continued regional instability and unpredictable outbursts of conflicts around the world, most often at the expense of the lives and properties of less fortunate groups and populations.

For example, the U.S. invasions of Afghanistan and Iraq had devastating consequences on the international system since the international community did not have the appropriate mechanisms or the wherewithal to find a peaceful resolution to the dispute between the parties following the invasion and overthrow of the regimes. Wars can be unavoidable, but even then, the international community has lacked the capacity to forge a framework for the parameters of the conflict. What has transpired instead have been "unending wars" with incalculable costs for these countries, the regions, and the international system itself. The lack of such a comprehensive mechanism for conflict resolution, which continues today, is not an oversight, but a conscious choice by the big powers to perpetuate their privileged positions in the international system. It should not need reminding that this structure could not have achieved peace and stability either in Afghanistan or Iraq. Instead, in both war-ravaged countries, we find broken political systems and continued confrontations between different social groups that do not bode well for the future of peace and stability in the region. When the strongest nations leverage their power in the international organizations to achieve an outcome most beneficial to themselves instead of international peace and security, conflicts persist and perpetuate unstable regions virtually condemned to exist in a lack of peace.

In Syria and Yemen (among others), for instance, the big powers prioritized their national interests and geopolitical prerogatives rather than uniting around the purpose of ending these conflicts. In fact, these conflicts became proxy wars between global and regional actors, resulting in humanitarian disasters of historic proportions. As Western countries refused to intervene in Syria to protect civilians from the Assad regime's unspeakable war crimes (though having done just that in Libya a few months earlier), some other states saw a geopolitical opportunity to ensure the continuation of the regime and were enabled by their partners and allies at the UNSC. There has been no serious resolution passed by the UNSC against the regime's atrocities against civilians or the millions of IDPs and refugees. In Yemen, the support by regional actors to various groups proved fatal, resulting in humanitarian tragedies for years now. In this case as well, the U.S. only recently under the Biden administration decided to stop providing arms to regional states that could end up being used in the civil war in Yemen. Once again, the international conflict resolution mechanisms were not only inadequate to resolve the underlying conflict between different warring parties, but the international powers' geopolitical calculations overrode international humanitarian efforts and worsened the crisis at many different levels.

In Cyprus, the UN efforts to find a resolution to the Cyprus issue under Secretary-General Kofi Annan's plan were rejected by the Greek Cypriots and regardless of this, the European Union unwisely and inexplicably admitted the Greek Administration of Southern Cyprus as a full member. The EU's foreign policy institutions failed to coordinate with the UN to produce an equitable solution. The frozen conflict in Karabakh created a status quo where Armenia's invasion of Azerbaijani lands was sustained over the course of several decades. It continued until recently and ended after the military operations of Azerbaijan. When pro-Russian forces annexed Crimea and threatened further military action along Ukraine's border, once again, the international community was unable to find a solution to the conflict due to the ineffectiveness of international conflict resolution mechanisms and great power politics in the region. In conflict after conflict, the international community has proven woefully inadequate, unprepared, and underfunded to deal with these crises.

Türkiye, however, has pursued a drastically different approach to conflict resolution and has adopted a stability and peace first approach, believing that its national interest would be furthered by the resolution of international conflicts. It is a familiar cliché about Türkiye living in a tough neighborhood with ongoing regional conflicts,[1] but this continues to be applicable. Every single neighbor of the country is either engaged in conflict or a major border dispute that could easily evolve into conflict. The Cyprus issue continues to be a frozen conflict that has become more difficult to resolve with each passing decade. Syria has been on the verge of collapse, having produced millions of internally displaced persons (IDPs) and refugees. Iraq continues to suffer from the fallout from the U.S. invasion in 2003. Iran is being treated as a rogue state by the West and lives under constant threat of attack by the U.S. and covert attacks by Israel. Armenia remains in conflict with Azerbaijan, despite the recent liberation of the Nagorno-Karabakh region by Azerbaijani forces. Russia continues to occupy Crimea and parts of Ukraine. Türkiye continues to struggle against international terrorism and domestic terror groups in a region rife with conflict and instability. Despite all these adverse conditions, Türkiye persists in working toward resolving conflicts by engaging all legitimate actors that are interested in resolving conflicts and by trying to launch international initiatives in its neighborhood.

Faced with the fallout and secondary effects of conflicts in its neighborhood, Türkiye has often been left alone in confronting international challenges. Seeking a stable and peaceful environment to advance its national interests, Türkiye has regularly conducted diplomacy in a way to resolve rather than exacerbate conflicts. Türkiye has often had to deal with the cost of the failures of the international community. Conflict resolution studies often posit that it is important for a country to be a neutral, disinterested party to the conflict in order to make a serious contribution toward ending it. However, it may not be constructive to stay neutral when one of the parties commits ethnic cleansing and massacres against its own people. These conflicts also have the potential to export insecurities towards the region and destabilize its entirety. Türkiye has observed that in the region, civil wars are like wildfires that endanger not only human life but also stability across the borders. Civil wars spread radicalization and extremism across borders. These civil wars bring all forms of illegal activities to the region, including arms and human smuggling. Thus, it would be in the best interest of the nations to engage in policies that would resolve the conflicts in a timely manner and prevent the spread of the conflicts and insecurities across the borders.

Türkiye has confirmed this as a result of the conflicts around its borders. Both as a stabilizing and a stability-seeking power, Türkiye can leverage its democratic system, open market, economic resources, and security partnerships to contribute to regional conflict resolution efforts. Türkiye is astute to this fact and has sought to resolve conflicts to allow for mutual interests to emerge naturally rather than exploit them for narrow self-interest. Whereas the international community too often fails in providing solutions to conflicts, Türkiye consistently pushes for diplomacy and engagement with a view toward achieving stability and peace. Türkiye has recognized that serious investment in conflict resolution is not simply a choice to gain accolades in the eyes of the international community but a basic requirement of Türkiye's own national security and interests in one of the most unstable regions of the world. This chapter focuses on Türkiye's conflict resolution efforts through several examples to highlight the country's unique contributions to peace and stability in its region in an increasingly uncertain and disorderly world.

The Cyprus Issue: It Takes Two to Tango

When the AK Party came to power in the early 2000s, it immediately pushed for a comprehensive reform agenda including full European Union (EU) membership. This was done both to contribute to regional stability and to improve Turkish democracy at home. The new government led the way in rethinking Türkiye's long-standing foreign policy issues[2] such as the Cyprus issue. The resolution of this decades-old conflict through a mutual agreement between the Turkish Cypriots in the north and Greek Cypriots in the south promised to help bring stability and peace to the region. The Turkish government under then prime minister Erdoğan was committed to this goal from the beginning even at the risk of political backlash at home. The AK Party government pushed for a fresh approach. As Cyprus had been a cornerstone of Turkish foreign policy, the AK Party's new approach amounted to nothing less than a restructuring of the Cyprus policy.[3]

A resolution to the conflict through UN-sponsored talks would not only pave the way for lasting peace but also allow the island to eventually become part of the EU under the Annan Plan. The plan called for a bizonal federal structure comprising two states, one in the north and another in the south segment of the island, a Turkish-Cypriot and a Greek-Cypriot state, respectively.[4] In this way, peace and stability in Cyprus and the Mediterranean overlapped with Turkish national interests in a way that made the AK Party's argument for a solution even more potent. Notwithstanding the pitfalls and potential domestic political backlash, Prime Minister Erdoğan adopted a courageous posture in Cyprus, pushing for a solution upon which both communities on the island could agree.

Under these conditions, 65% of Turkish Cypriots voted to accept the Annan Plan, but 76% of Greek Cypriots rejected it. Turkish leadership at the time spent a good amount of time and energy in producing a feasible solution and finally had agreed to support the Annan Plan. While the Turkish side crafted a coherent approach around a political solution through the Annan Plan, the Greek Cypriot political leadership put forth little effort to convince their constituencies, who saw the plan as a win for the Turkish side. The referendum in the south was couched in confusing ballot language and the failure of the Greek Cypriot leadership to embrace the proposal ensured the rejection by voters representing the Greek Cypriot position.[5]

Prime Minister Erdoğan had taken a significant political risk, but the Greek Cypriots felt no serious pressure from Greece and rejected the plan only to be rewarded with immediate EU membership. This was arguably one of the EU's worst strategic decisions as the union's own laws preclude extending membership to countries with unresolved border issues. The EU rewarded the Greek Cypriots with full membership for the entire island although the island remained divided. The consequences of this misguided decision have been to deepen the resistance against resolving a frozen conflict and to alienate Türkiye further from Europe. Türkiye did not give up on its EU membership bid despite the double standard at work on the issue. But the country has suffered from a virtually immovable roadblock before its EU membership talks. Greek Cypriots believed that they had leverage over the north, as they were on the cusp of becoming a full EU member without the need to compromise with Turkish Cypriots.[6]

Fast forward to the current moment, Türkiye has recently reasserted its rights in the Eastern Mediterranean, contravening the claims by Greece in the Aegean Sea and by Greek Cypriots around the island of Cyprus.[7] Some observers have noted that the development of hydrocarbon resources in the Mediterranean cannot be fully realized without Türkiye and in the absence of a comprehensive political solution. Turkish leadership saw, years ago, the need to resolve the conflict, but the Greek Cypriots, emboldened by the EU, declined a solution that would have benefited all parties in the long run. Such a lack of strategic foresight has vexed the region and exacerbated tensions in the geopolitical neighborhood. This episode shows that Türkiye's contribution to regional peace and stability using international conflict resolution mechanisms has been robust, but nevertheless has been hampered by a lack of vision by other parties such as Greece and Greek Cypriots, not to mention the EU. Even after the referendum on the Annan Plan, there were calls for Türkiye to compromise further and perhaps "sweeten the deal"[8] on the resolution of the dispute, but lasting conflict resolution requires willing parties who perceive benefits around a long-term vision of peace and stability. Despite Turkish efforts over the years, this has been the reality that has defined the Cyprus issue, and the result has been a difficult and dangerous geostrategic situation in the Eastern Mediterranean.

Syria: Türkiye's Foray into the Middle East

Until the arrival of the Arab Spring in Syria in 2011, Türkiye's policy toward Syria was a successful example of conflict resolution through rebuilding political ties with a neighbor. Pursuing the goal of regional integration through policies such as cross-border trade and visa liberalization, Türkiye deepened its ties with its southern neighbor. The Turkish view on Syria shared the U.S. concerns over support for terrorism and the proliferation of weapons of mass destruction. But Türkiye also judged that further militarization of the region would be a recipe for disaster. Instead, Türkiye suggested that the integration of Syria into the region through commerce and diplomacy would help build peace and stability.

The Turkish political establishment had been deeply troubled about Syria for a long time given the PKK's base of operations in the Bekaa Valley in the 1980s and especially in the 1990s. In the late 1990s, Türkiye even undertook a show of force against Syria by amassing troops along the Syrian border, which led to the departure of the PKK leader Ocalan from Syria and his eventual capture. With such a history of enmity between the two countries, a fresh, new approach brought on by the AK Party government at the time led to a fundamentally different type of relations. In the wake of the promise of a new Syria with the succession in the country's leadership from Hafez al-Assad to his son Bashar al-Assad, Türkiye wanted to ensure its southern neighbor would not revert to its old ways. Syria was deeply isolated and a host to several clandestine operations by various countries on its soil. The country had been maintaining a certain status quo in its relations with Israel. Diplomacy, engagement, and conflict resolution appeared to be a must for the new Turkish foreign policy in the early 2000s.

Under the new AK Party government, Türkiye implemented policies of engagement and openness toward Syria that made trade and tourism much easier while cultivating close political relations with Bashar al-Assad. The cross-border activities improved the local economies of both countries and visa-free travel allowed an unprecedented flow of people as well as goods and services. Turkish efforts to build influence and shape the country's overall direction in the long run were largely successful and were even appreciated by the international community. The Syrian leadership, for its part, had an interest in opening to its northern neighbor both for economic reasons and for broader political acceptance by the West. Strengthening relations with Türkiye was not domestically costly for the Syrian leadership, which would have had a harder time garnering support for a quick opening to the West, especially the U.S. Türkiye, for its part, did not build influence simply for national interest but also for broader regional stability. Positioning itself as a reliable interlocutor between Syria and the West, Türkiye's engagement allowed the Syrian regime to consider options outside some of its traditional allies.

The best example of Türkiye's efforts to use its political influence and diplomatic clout occurred when the Turkish leadership mediated talks between Syria and Israel.[9] The two countries found a neutral partner in Türkiye that could facilitate negotiations.[10] The last round of talks between Israel and Syria over the Golan Heights under U.S. auspices ended without any results in 2000. The Turkish mediation efforts, which were revealed to the public in 2008, resulted from the fact that both countries had good relations with Türkiye at the time.[11] Türkiye hosted numerous rounds of secret negotiations between Syria and Israel, bringing the two sides to the cusp of a historic agreement. Turkish diplomacy was disciplined and serious with no leaks to the media on such a sensitive issue that could have resolved one of the most important frozen conflicts in the region. Given the skeptical Turkish domestic views about either country, then Prime Minister Erdoğan's vision for peace and political capital spent on diplomacy was innovative and groundbreaking by any measure. A serious conflict resolution strategy required the discipline, seriousness, and innovation that Erdoğan displayed throughout the whole process.

Turkish investment in Syria under Bashar al-Assad in the early 2000s appeared imminently poised to yield returns in the form of a peace agreement and a rapprochement between two hostile countries that would end a long-standing conflict in the region. Türkiye's mediation efforts in the Syrian-Israeli conflict, however, were interrupted by Israel's abruptly launched heavy-handed military operations in Gaza. There was no advance notice of any type of hostilities and Gaza had already been experiencing serious humanitarian challenges. The Turkish government could not simply look the other way. Erdoğan directly criticized the Israeli leadership for attacking Gaza[12] while negotiating with Syria through Türkiye's mediating role to help contribute to regional stability and peace.[13] The Israeli-Syrian potential rapprochement ended because of the Israeli government's military operations in Gaza. Türkiye was willing to use its political clout with Syria for the benefit of peace in the region, but by virtue of its own principled stance was unwilling to look the other way when Israel attacked Palestinians. Nevertheless, Türkiye showed that it is ready to contribute to conflict resolution in its region especially when there are willing parties.

Turkish Commitment to Intercommunal Dialogue in Iraq

Türkiye was adversely impacted by the First Gulf War and its regional consequences. Türkiye received around half a million refugees and had to resolve difficult security issues as a result. The PKK terror attacks inside Türkiye spiked in the early 1990s. The no-fly zone established by the international coalition in northern Iraq created a safe haven for the Iraqi Kurds over time, but it also resulted in a relatively weaker authority that could not address the PKK situation. As a result, Türkiye was vulnerable to cross-border terror activity by the PKK. The conflict next door created a dangerous situation with unprecedented security challenges, even as Türkiye had joined the U.S.-led international coalition.[14] Hundreds of thousands of refugees from northern Iraq ended up in the southeast of Türkiye.

This memory guided, at least to a certain extent, the Turkish public's opposition to the U.S. invasion of Iraq in 2003. Facing U.S. pressure and offers for financial help, the Turkish parliament rejected the Bush administration's request to open a northern front from Türkiye to enable Iraq's invasion.[15] Although this decision marked a low point in the history of Turkish-American relations, Türkiye still played a role in the immediate aftermath of the invasion by allowing coalition flights over its airspace. Türkiye cooperated with the United States on issues such as international counterterrorism efforts and political inclusion inside Iraq. Despite the relative ease of the initial stages of the invasion, the security situation deteriorated significantly with the "de-Baathification" process to rid the Iraqi state institutions of former Saddam regime elements.[16]

The disastrous long-term consequences of this decision became clear to everyone,[17] especially in the mid-2000s, as violence reached new heights. The Sunni groups believed they had been robbed of their power and status, as they ended up in the minority without a power-sharing agreement including the majority Shia groups.

The U.S. failure to keep the Iraqi state intact and secure a political compact between the Shia and Sunni groups[18] fomented a ripe environment for the rise of radicalism and extremist terrorism. Al-Qaeda in Iraq became even more prominent than its original terror organization in Afghanistan and the seeds of more than a decade of struggle were sown at that moment. Large numbers of Sunni populations were pushed out of the political system by the Shia groups. Türkiye emerged as a positive influence over the Turkomans[19] and Sunni groups with which it had some relations. Türkiye encouraged their participation in the drafting of the constitution and in election processes to achieve stability in the country. Türkiye opposed policies of leaders like al-Maliki,[20] whose platform promised little to nothing for Sunnis and offered no clear path for their inclusion in the political system. No power-sharing and oil revenue-sharing agreement proved stable and long-lasting, as intermittent rounds of violence broke out frequently. The U.S. failed to offer a formula for long-term peace and stability.[21]

Türkiye, nevertheless, tried to encourage and facilitate intercommunal dialogue and political inclusion while also maintaining its ties to all segments of the political spectrum. The Sunni political establishment had been sidelined because of the invasion and the U.S. de-Baathification efforts ended up alienating large segments of Iraqi society. The ideological imposition of a nation-building effort and drawing up political agreements based on ethnic differences would become a recipe for disaster. If large portions of Iraqi society were to be pushed out of the system, it would create an unsustainable situation and lead to further disintegration of the country. Türkiye understood this and worked with all political forces in Iraq to ensure that everyone engaged in the political process, regardless how flawed it may have been.

Iraq's invasion had regional reverberations and global implications, and working only through domestic national forces for the country's stability was not going to be enough. The rebuilding of the political system and the reconstruction of the country required a broad international coalition of like-minded countries. Based on this understanding and perspective, Türkiye convened the group of "Friends of Iraq" to engage regional and global actors with a stake in stability and peace in the country.[22] Türkiye's efforts were comprehensive since then prime minister Erdoğan understood that just as inclusion and continued participation of different Iraqi groups were essential, international support for reconstruction was also crucial.

Türkiye became a real force of stability in the northern region of the country when it established strong ties with the Kurdistan Regional Government (KRG).[23] While Türkiye's security and energy priorities laid the groundwork for this opening,[24] it still was a courageous political decision by Prime Minister Erdoğan. Turkish public opinion harbored suspicion toward the KRG because of the security challenges emanating from Iraq throughout the 1990s and 2000s. The AK Party under Erdoğan's leadership was able to convince the Turkish public and the security establishment of the benefits of establishing good relations with the KRG. This has proven to be an underappreciated and understudied successful case study of conflict resolution. It is often described as an instance of Turkish pragmatism in favor of national interest. But Türkiye has also been guided by the need for economic integration and security cooperation for the sake of regional stability and peace. The Turkish approach to northern Iraq did not exclude acknowledging its relations with the rest of Iraq. On the contrary, convinced that stability and peace could only come from good relations with all Iraqi groups, Türkiye made sure to strengthen its ties with the new Baghdad government, along with Sunni and Turkmen groups in addition to Iraqi Kurds in the north. Once again, Türkiye put its good relations with all Iraqi parties to good use by encouraging and facilitating dialogue between them, recognizing that it required different strategies to deal with different groups in Iraq's more loosely defined federal structure. Nevertheless, Türkiye did not lose sight of the importance of the country's overall integrity.

Türkiye's Mediation Efforts on the Iran Nuclear Issue

The Iran nuclear issue has consumed the Middle East for more than a decade as the international community sought ways to restrict Iran's ability to develop a nuclear weapon and maintain "normal" relations with the country. Major powers have spent years negotiating with Iran to secure an agreement that would preclude the country from ever acquiring a nuclear weapon. At the same time, having a nuclear program has been a difficult issue in the case of Iran because the international community could never really be confident about Iran's exact intentions. Iran's nuclear activities continued with periods of heightened tensions, sanctions, and even signs of imminent conflict at times.[25] Türkiye has always sought an accommodation that would prevent the region from plunging into yet another era of war and destruction. As a country with centuries-old relations with Iran as its next-door neighbor as well as its regional rival on certain issues, Türkiye has a national security interest in ensuring a peaceful resolution of the standoff between Iran and the rest of the international community.

While President George W. Bush had listed Iran as part of the "axis of evil," President Obama had promised to reach out to Iran to resolve the long-standing nuclear issue.[26] When he began his administration in 2009, Obama conducted dual track diplomacy[27] by seeking to impose sanctions on Iran through the UN Security Council (UNSC) while exploring ways to arrive at a deal. Türkiye was a non-permanent member of the UNSC at the time and offered to help mediate between the international community and Iran. At the time, diplomatic channels were largely closed with only some secret channels open to gauge the Iranian response. Following Obama encouraging Iran to agree to a swap deal that had failed in the past, Türkiye alongside Brazil (another non-permanent UNSC member at the time) lobbied Iran to accept the terms of the deal.[28] Iran refused to negotiate with the international community over the nuclear issues, arguing that it was the sovereign right of the country to enrich uranium and develop peaceful nuclear technology. Given the impending showdown, there was a real fear of a potential escalation and war.

Türkiye's robust diplomatic efforts at the time were not fully appreciated and there was an expectation among Western nations that Turkish mediation would fail. But Prime Minister Erdoğan's personal investment in the matter (i.e., he even visited Iran to conduct one-on-one meetings with the Iranian supreme leader Khamenei himself) produced a result that surprised many. Iran agreed to a deal to ship its highly enriched uranium to Türkiye in return for low enriched uranium to be used for civilian purposes. As the deal was struck near the deadline of impending sanctions by the UNSC, the U.S. chose to downplay the significance of the deal and argued that it was an Iranian ploy to avoid consequences. The U.S. had, in fact, encouraged Türkiye to follow through on its diplomatic efforts, but then refused to consider talks around the Tehran Declaration by Türkiye, Brazil, and Iran. Türkiye was deeply disappointed and voted against sanctions on Iran in June 2010,[29] arguing that it needed to stand by its signature on the Tehran Declaration. This created diplomatic friction between Türkiye and the United States, which expected Turkiye to abstain from voting. Türkiye not only invested political capital and diplomatic efforts in this process for regional stability, but also opposed Western efforts to escalate the situation.

The U.S. decision to push forward with sanctions meant that an international sanctions regime would have to be built and maintained with Russian and Chinese cooperation for a few years before Iran felt the pain of punitive measures and would finally relent to negotiations. It also meant the deep mistrust would continue and the hardliners in Iran could argue that the U.S. was solely interested in inflicting pain on the Iranian people rather than reaching an agreement. Even if this argument may not be valid, it did resonate among the Iranian public and many countries in the international community. As the U.S. built a sanctions regime after the summer of 2010, reaching an agreement would have to wait until Obama's second term, when a narrow nuclear deal was achieved in 2015. If Türkiye's efforts had been properly recognized and a diplomatic agreement had been forged, a deal could have come earlier, and Iran's nuclear program would not have progressed as much as it did in the ensuing years.

Living in the region that would be adversely affected by the sanctions regime, tensions, and potential escalation to war, Türkiye invested much diplomatic energy and political capital to solve a regional crisis. Turkish leadership saw that the only way to ensure Iran did not acquire a nuclear weapon was through diplomacy focused on the country's compliance rather than the pressure campaign. Türkiye's commitment to conflict resolution in its region on such a high-stakes standoff between the international community and Iran was exemplary, to say the least.

When the international community decided to move forward with the sanctions regime and refused to acknowledge Türkiye's constructive diplomatic efforts, Erdoğan said Türkiye had no choice but to honor the signature it had placed on the Tehran Declaration alongside Brazil. This was a first as Türkiye voted against sanctions that were championed by its NATO ally, the U.S., to bring Iran to the negotiations. Türkiye also defended rights, such as having a nuclear program, as they had been well established by international laws and norms. This was Türkiye's principled stance because the international community was seeking to use this right as a bargaining chip against Iran, thereby creating a double standard. Türkiye's capacity to enrich uranium was and is still non-existent, but Türkiye has also advocated for the norms and principles of the international system to be applied consistently. The denial of the Iranian right to enrichment and its use as a political bargaining chip in future negotiations were not consistent with constructive diplomacy. Türkiye saw that the only way to end the standoff between Iran and the international community was through good faith diplomacy and consistent implementation of international law.

Libya: Türkiye's National Interests Overlap with Regional Stability

Few countries proved to be immune to the effects of the Arab Spring and even fewer leaders in the Arab world were able to survive it by heeding the demands of their own people. When the Arab Spring reached Libya, the country's leader Muammar Qaddafi promised to exact unprecedented levels of punishment on those who rebelled against his regime instead of trying to reach a political deal with the opposition groups. He had run the country for decades through the manipulation of different factions against each other and weakened all civil society to prevent any potential challenge to his power. While the opposition seemed scattered and vulnerable to the regime's power, Libya's turmoil was too important to ignore for geopolitical and geoeconomic reasons. The country's oil resources made it a major player in the global energy markets and Arab countries saw an opportunity to rid themselves of Qaddafi to advance their own geoeconomic interests. When the opposition forces in the country called for outside help in the face of Qaddafi's promise of unprecedented violence, the Arab League called for the establishment of a no-fly zone over the country[30] and the international community decided to intervene with consequences that continue to this day. Türkiye's policy to the last minute was to try to find a political solution between Qaddafi and the opposition in order to prevent conflict and regional instability. Once again, the Turkish leadership demonstrated its long-standing commitment to conflict resolution through diplomacy for the sake of regional stability and peace.

In the early days of the uprising in Libya, the international community hesitated to act to protect civilians. The responsibility to protect (R2P) principle[31] had rarely been invoked in the past and there was little appetite by the U.S. and its European allies to conduct yet another military intervention in the Middle East. Türkiye had humanitarian and economic interests in Libya, and sought to protect them.[32] Türkiye conducted its largest humanitarian operation to repatriate some 20,000 Turkish citizens from Libya who were living in the country at the time of the unrest. Türkiye attempted to find a negotiated solution between the regime and the opposition in addition to its Western allies. When Turkish efforts proved unsuccessful due to Qaddafi's intransigence, Erdoğan called on the Libyan leader to resign.[33]

These attempts lasted until the very last minute, right before the start of the NATO operation. Türkiye supported the NATO mission on its non-military aspects[34] to avoid being seen by the Libyan people as a hostile nation. The international community was worried about a large-scale massacre against the opposition and civilians in Libya and the Arab League's call for humanitarian intervention would translate to a "low-cost" operation. The end of the regime marked the beginning of a long-term divided country, as Türkiye had warned. The opposition seemed in control at first, but then deep divisions emerged in the country, making national unity an increasingly unlikely outcome over the course of the past decade. Almost ten years after the regime change in Libya, there are still many uncertainties in the country. Türkiye has continued its principled stand to support a legitimate government that will bring unity to the country. Türkiye still works with the UN-recognized national government in Tripoli while various regional players like Russia, the UAE, and France[35] support divisive figures such as Khalifa Haftar. Türkiye's support for the UN-recognized Government of National Accord (GNA)[36] has prevented yet another round of conflict and division in the country. It has ensured the continuation of the GNA government and has rendered political negotiations a necessity. Haftar's forces have been prevented from simply taking over the legitimate government in Tripoli by force because of Türkiye's policy.[37] Once again, Türkiye's consistent policy to work against division, civil war, and instability in Libya has paid off as it has brought a semblance of stability to the country. The GNA has been strengthened militarily and politically, which has allowed it to make several agreements with outside countries. During Libya's decade-old instability and civil war, Türkiye emerged as a stabilizing force and sought to continue avenues for eventually resolving the conflict through its military, political, and diplomatic capabilities.

The Syrian Civil War: The Arab Spring Turns to Winter on Türkiye's Doorstep

When the Arab Spring arrived in Syria, Türkiye had already been standing with the people's power movements following its policy that the continuation of authoritarian systems in the region was unsustainable. Without major reform and a new pact between undemocratic regimes and their peoples, instability and conflict would be unavoidable. Türkiye's rationale for calling on the Mubarak regime in Egypt and the Qaddafi regime in Libya to negotiate, implement reform, and create responsive political space for the opposition was informed by the following assessment: administrations that do not reflect the will of the people cannot survive in the long run. The Arab Spring had just shown that people's participation in the political system, their demand for reform, and their fight for dignity were knocking on the door of authoritarian systems. There was no way out for these regimes and if they wanted to survive, they needed to reform fast. This was Türkiye's advice to Assad in Syria as well. Türkiye did not stand idly by but worked for some nine months to convince the regime to implement meaningful change. Türkiye had cultivated a working relationship with Assad in the previous decade, and it used its influence to push for reform before things became extremely ugly, so to speak. Despite international and strong American pressure to take an immediate stance against Assad, Türkiye tried to leverage its political influence for conflict resolution purposes. But the Assad regime not only failed to heed Türkiye's advice, but also responded to peaceful protests with force. Once the regime attacked its own people brazenly in the month of Ramadan in August 2011, Türkiye decided to cut its ties with the regime and called for the end of Assad's rule.[38]

Over the next few years, Türkiye led international efforts to end the conflict. Ankara convened multiple different international conferences, summits, and gatherings in order to find a diplomatic solution to the problem. Türkiye continued to advocate for the rights of minorities and the demands of the opposition while calling for international intervention.[39] The international community's response was largely ineffective and resulted in the displacement of millions of Syrians. The regional instability and waves of terrorism threats coming out of Syria reached unmanageable proportions, as the country witnessed the worst humanitarian crisis to date in the 21st century. Türkiye's push for support of the opposition[40] and a multilateral intervention to prevent the Assad regime from committing more crimes against humanity were ignored in the West. While the Obama administration appeared willing to consider support for the opposition and drafted plans with Türkiye to provide military training and arms, President Obama changed his mind in the eleventh hour and backed away from potentially changing the balance of power on the ground. When Obama refused to support the opposition in a serious way in 2012 and 2013, the dynamics on the ground shifted in an irreversible way where the Assad regime gained confidence in being unconstrained in the war it had waged on its own people.

The Syrian conflict was transformed from an uprising against the regime to a civil war between many factions and international terror groups. The international community focused on terrorist groups and the Assad regime was given a pass even though it was terrorizing its own civilian population. The regime also used international terror groups to divide the opposition and tell the world that the real problem in Syria was terrorism, not the absence of representative government, political rights, or regime violence that it had instigated. This shift was crucial as it allowed for the conflict to turn into a protracted civil war that needed to be contained rather than resolved through international action. Türkiye's advocacy and diplomatic efforts to revise this perception and the regime's crimes were not sufficient to mobilize the international community. While pushing for international intervention, Türkiye also opened its doors to Syrian refugees to alleviate humanitarian suffering.

The international community's lack of focus and "catastrophic failure"[41] in ending the Syrian civil war abruptly shifted in the late summer and fall of 2014 when DAESH captured the Iraqi city of Mosul and ventured into Syria to establish its so-called caliphate.[42] In an effort to respond largely to the gruesome images coming out of Iraq, the Obama administration decided to support the PKK's Syrian extension, the YPG, to fight DAESH on the ground.[43]

With the Russian intervention in Syria in the fall of 2015, the general picture of the conflict changed one more time.[44] Türkiye also decided to intervene to clear its border from terror groups (DAESH and YPG/PKK) in August 2016 with its first troop deployment in the Syrian conflict.[45] Now that the Western allies refused to address the overall crisis and worked at cross purposes with Türkiye by supporting the PKK on the ground in northern Syria, the Turkish leadership saw no other way but to intervene militarily while continuing its diplomatic efforts to resolve the conflict and to alleviate the humanitarian crisis on the ground. Through the Astana and Sochi processes, Türkiye engaged with Russia and Iran in order to provide humanitarian assistance for the Syrians in the Idlib region. [46] This was not a choice for Türkiye but instead a necessity. At the same time, Türkiye tied its diplomatic efforts to the end goal of arriving at a political settlement through the UN resolutions. Despite military coordination with Russia, Türkiye still called on Western allies to address the situation on the ground in Syria. Exhibiting a lack of strategic foresight and an unwillingness to spend much effort except to prevent migrants from arriving on the continent, Europeans were unhelpful. The Obama administration was focused only on the DAESH threat and adopted a misguided policy to fight against international terrorism. Under these conditions, Türkiye sought to secure its national interest which overlapped with the end of the Syrian civil war.

From the very beginning, Türkiye engaged the Assad regime for a resolution to the emerging conflict. When the regime refused to heed the demands of its own people and resorted to violence, Türkiye had to abandon its months-long efforts to create a political reform process. From then onward, Türkiye called on the international community for action in Syria to stop the regime's massacres and the impending humanitarian catastrophe. It called on its Western allies to support the opposition and create safe zones inside the country to protect civilians. Türkiye also created the "Friends of Syria" group to prevent the regime from further destabilizing the country and to help bring an end to the conflict. Western allies refused to forge an international coalition to intervene in Syria, which resulted in the creation of millions of IDPs and refugees. Türkiye was often left alone in its calls for intervention in Syria, and actors such as Russia and Iran became major players. Türkiye supported the UN-sponsored Geneva process as well, but the conflict was prolonged in the absence of a political solution. When Russia and Iran emerged as the main actors in the absence of Western intervention, Türkiye engaged those actors through the Sochi and Astana processes in order to protect civilians. Thanks to these Turkish efforts, millions of civilians have been protected and the Assad regime has been unable to claim total victory. The situation in Syria remains dire and Türkiye continues to recognize that there is a need for a robust political engagement on the part of international actors. As we recently passed the tenth anniversary of the outbreak of the conflict, Türkiye is still trying to engage the international community through its conflict resolution efforts.

Türkiye, under the leadership of Erdoğan since the 2000s, has been at the forefront of international efforts to resolve conflicts in its region and around the world. Türkiye has sought to prevent conflicts from emerging in the first place, broker agreements between parties in conflicts, resolve long-standing frozen conflicts, and manage the dangerous impact of ongoing conflicts. Türkiye has not waited for the international community to act and provide solutions, which were too often skewed toward protecting the regional interests of the great powers rather than bringing about peace in the region. As a regional power with an open economy, Türkiye has invested a significant amount of diplomatic energy and national resources to help build stability and peace in its neighborhood. This has been considered by Turkish policymakers to be both in the national interest and for the benefit of a region suffering from decades of war and conflict. Ankara has sought a relatively stable environment to promote its business interests, build political relationships, and foster goodwill among the peoples of the region. Türkiye's principled and consistent efforts to manage crises and resolve conflicts have produced major results and allowed the country to claim moral high ground when it comes to promulgating humanitarian policies. In contrast, the international system has failed to produce effective conflict resolution mechanisms to end the conflicts and disputes among nations, ethnic groups, and states.

The case studies discussed in this chapter show clearly that Türkiye has pursued a conflict resolution approach that acknowledges these considerations. In stark contrast to the "national interest first" approach of many powerful nations, Türkiye has insisted on working to achieve peace and stability that would in turn serve its national interest. Türkiye always seeks to mediate in order to find a peaceful resolution in conflicts, be they invasions, annexations, civil wars, or regional power struggles. Unlike nations that seek status and power primarily through implementation of a naked self-interest policy, Türkiye consistently approaches international conflicts through a vision of bringing about stability to further its national goals. There need not be a contradiction between furthering a nation's national interest and seeking peace and stability. International actors who seek to destabilize regions and manipulate the power struggles for their own national interests fail to provide a semblance of stability around the world. In fact, such a misguided policy simply contributes to the deterioration of conflicts, the deepening of humanitarian crises, and the prolonging of wars around the world.

ENDNOTES

1 Kirişci, Kemal, "Turkey's Engagement with Its Neighborhood: A 'Synthetic' and Multidimensional Look at Turkey's Foreign Policy Transformation," *Turkish Studies* 13 (3): 319-41, 2012, https://doi.org/10.1080/14683849.2012.717444.

2 Müftüler Baç, Meltem, "Turkey's Political Reforms and the Impact of the European Union," *South European Society and Politics* 10 (1): 17–31, 2005, https://doi.org/10.1080/13608740500037916.

3 Çelenk, Ayşe Aslihan, "The Restructuring of Turkey's Policy towards Cyprus: The Justice and Development Party's Struggle for Power," *Turkish Studies* 8 (3): 349–63, 2007, https://doi.org/10.1080/14683840701489092.

4 Sözen, Ahmet and Kudret Özersay, "The Annan Plan: State Succession or Continuity," *Middle Eastern Studies* 43 (1): 125–41, 2007, https://doi.org/10.1080/00263200601079773.

5 Dodd, Clement, *The History and Politics of the Cyprus Conflict*, Palgrave Macmillan UK, 2010, https://doi.org/10.1057/9780230275287.

6 Tocci, "Reflections on Post-referendum Cyprus."

7 "The Eastern Mediterranean Tinderbox: Why Greek-Turkish Rivalries Have Expanded," BBC News, August 25, 2020, sec. Europe, https://www.bbc.com/news/world-europe-53906360.

8 Tocci, "Reflections on Post-referendum Cyprus."

9 Allah, Milad Alodet, "An Account of the 2008 Syrian–Israeli Negotiations in Turkey," *Contemporary Arab Affairs* 9 (1): 100–114, 2016, https://doi.org/10.1080/17550912.2015.1118208.

10 Altunisik, Meliha and Esra Cuhadar, "Turkey's Search for a Third Party Role in Arab–Israeli Conflicts: A Neutral Facilitator or a Principal Power Mediator?" *Mediterranean Politics* 15 (3): 371–92, 2010, https://doi.org/10.1080/13629395.2010.517101.

11 Walker, Peter, "Syria and Israel Officially Confirm Peace Talks," *The Guardian*, May 21, 2008, http://www.theguardian.com/world/2008/may/21/israelandthepalestinians.syria.

12 Bennhold, Katrin, "Leaders of Turkey and Israel Clash at Davos Panel," *The New York Times*, January 29, 2009, sec. World, https://www.nytimes.com/2009/01/30/world/europe/30clash.html.

13 "Turkey Offers to Resume Israel-Syria Mediation," Reuters, January 29, 2010, sec. World News, https://www.reuters.com/article/us-Turkey-israel-idUSTRE60S59420100129.

14 Brown, Cameron S., "Turkey in the Gulf Wars of 1991 and 2003," *Turkish Studies* 8 (1): 85–119, 2007, https://doi.org/10.1080/14683840601162054.

15 "Turkey Rejects U.S. Troop Proposal - Mar. 1, 2003," CNN, n.d.,

https://www.cnn.com/2003/WORLD/meast/03/01/sprj.irq.main/.

16 Diamond, Larry, "What Went Wrong in Iraq," *Foreign Affairs* 83 (5): 34–56, 2004, https://doi.org/10.2307/20034066.

17 Sissons, Miranda and Abdulrazzaq Al-Saeidi, "Iraq's de-Baathification Still Haunts the Country," Aljazeera, n.d., https://www.aljazeera.com/opinions/2013/3/12/iraqs-de-baathification-still-haunts-the-country.

18 Byman, Daniel, "An Autopsy of the Iraq Debacle: Policy Failure or Bridge Too Far?" *Security Studies* 17 (4): 599–643, 2008, https://doi.org/10.1080/09636410802507974.

19 Strakes, Jason E., "Current Political Complexities of the Iraqi Turkmen," *Iran & the Caucasus* 13 (2): 365–82, 2009, https://www.jstor.org/stable/25703815.

20 "No Need to Give More Right to Speak to Iraqi Pm," Anadolu Agency, April 22, 2012, https://www.aa.com.tr/en/Turkey/no-need-to-give-more-right-to-speak-to-iraqi-pm/372095.

21 Scahill, Jeremy and Murtaza Hussain, "The Changing of the Overlords: From the Rubble of the U.S. War in Iraq, Iran Built a New Order," *The Intercept* (blog), November 18, 2019, https://theintercept.com/2019/11/18/us-iraq-invasion-iran/.

22 "Annan to Meet with 'Group of Friends' of Iraq to Chart Way Forward," UN News, February 18, 2004, https://news.un.org/en/story/2004/02/94442-annan-meet-group-friends-iraq-chart-way-forward.

23 Shadid, Anthony, "Resurgent Turkey Flexes Its Muscles Around Iraq," *The New York Times*, January 5, 2011, sec. World, https://www.nytimes.com/2011/01/05/world/middleeast/05turkey.html.

24 Wahab, Bilal, "Iraq and KRG Energy Policies: Actors, Challenges and Opportunities," Foreign Policy Initiative, n.d., https://policycommons.net/artifacts/1478837/iraq-and-krg-energy-policies/2137779/.

25 Burr, William, "A Brief History of U.S.-Iranian Nuclear Negotiations," *Bulletin of the Atomic Scientists* 65 (1): 21–34, 2009, https://doi.org/10.2968/065001004.

26 Murray, Donette, "The Carcass of Dead Policies: Lessons for Obama in Dealing with Iran," *Contemporary Politics* 16 (2): 209–23, 2010, https://doi.org/10.1080/13569771003783992.

27 Üstün, Kadir, "Turkey Iran Policy: Between Diplomacy and Sanctions," *Insight Turkey* 12 (3): 19–26, 2010, https://www.jstor.org/stable/26334100

28 Crail, Peter, "Brazil, Turkey Broker Fuel Swap with Iran | Arms Control Association," 2021, https://www.armscontrol.org/act/2010-06/brazil-Turkey-broker-fuel-swap-iran.

29 "Security Council Imposes Additional Sanctions on Iran, Voting 12 in Favour to 2 Against, with 1 Abstention | Meetings Coverage and Press Releases," UN Security Council, June 9, 2010, https://www.un.org/press/en/2010/sc9948.doc.htm.

30 Leiby, Richard and Muhammad Mansour, "Arab League Asks U.N. for No-Fly Zone over Libya," *The Washington Post*, March 12, 2011, sec. World, https://www.washingtonpost.com/world/arab-league-asks-un-for-no-fly-zone-over-libya/2011/03/12/ABoieOR_story.html.

31 Thakur, Ramesh, "Libya and the Responsibility to Protect: Between Opportunistic Humanitarianism and Value-Free Pragmatism," *Security Challenges* 7 (4): 13–25, 2011.https://www.jstor.org/stable/26467113?seq=1#metadata_info_tab_contents.

32 "Turkey Opposes Any NATO Operation in Libya," Reuters, March 14, 2011, sec. Editor's Picks, https://www.reuters.com/article/us-libya-Turkey-idUSTRE72D49D20110314.

33 "Turkey's PM Erdoğan Urges Col Muammar Gaddafi to Quit," BBC News, May 3, 2011, sec. Europe, https://www.bbc.com/news/world-europe-13265825.

34 "Turkey Reluctantly Joins NATO Operations against Libya," France 24, March 24, 2011, https://www.france24.com/en/20110324-Turkey-allows-nato-command-libya-military-operations-vote.

35 Necat Tasci, Ufuk, "How the UAE, Russia and France Have Teamed up in Libya," 2020, https://www.trtworld.com/magazine/how-the-uae-russia-and-france-have-teamed-up-in-libya-42583.

36 "Erdoğan Says Turkey Aims to Boost Ties with Libya's GNA," Reuters, October 4, 2020, sec. Emerging Markets, https://www.reuters.com/article/us-libya-security-Turkey-idUSKBN26P0Z3.

37 Allinson, Tom, "Libya: Turkish Strategy Leaves Haftar on the Defensive | DW | 07.05.2020," Deutsche Welle, July 5, 2020, https://www.dw.com/en/libya-turkish-strategy-leaves-haftar-on-the-defensive/a-53365043.

38 "Turkish PM Calls on Syria's Assad to Quit," Reuters, November 22, 2011, sec. World News, https://www.reuters.com/article/us-Turkey-syria-idUSTRE7AL0WJ20111122.

39 Tisdall, Simon, "Türkiye Calls on Major Powers to Intervene in Syria," *The Guardian*, October 19, 2012, http://www.theguardian.com/world/2012/oct/19/Turkey-britain-us-intervene-syria.

40 Stack, Liam, "In Slap at Syria, Turkey Shelters Anti-Assad Fighters," *The New York Times*, October 27, 2011, sec. World, https://www.nytimes.com/2011/10/28/world/europe/turkey-is-sheltering-antigovernment-syrian-militia.html

41 "Syria: Seven Years of Catastrophic Failure by the International Community," March 15, 2018, https://www.amnesty.org/en/latest/news/2018/03/syria-seven-years-of-catastrophic-failure-by-the-international-community/.

42 Abdulrazaq, Tallha and Gareth Stansfield, "The Enemy Within: DAESH and the Conquest of Mosul," *The Middle East Journal* 70 (4): 525–42, 2016, https://www.jstor.org/stable/26427457.

43 Zenko, Micah, "What Obama Really Meant by 'No Boots on the Ground,'" The Atlantic, December 3, 2015, https://www.theatlantic.com/international/archive/2015/12/obama-boots-on-the-ground/418635/.

44 Charap, Samuel, Elina Treyger, and Edward Geist, "Understanding Russia's Intervention in Syria," October 2019, https://www.rand.org/pubs/research_reports/RR3180.html.

45 Arango, Tim, Anne Barnard, and Ceylan Yeginsu, "Turkey's Military Plunges into Syria, Enabling Rebels to Capture DAESH Stronghold," *The New York Times*, August 24, 2016, sec. World, https://www.nytimes.com/2016/08/25/world/middleeast/Turkey-syria-isis.html.

46 Namli, Kaan and Fadi Farasin, "Astana: The Rise of a New Alliance and Its Implications for International Relations" in *The Syrian Crisis: Effects on the Regional and International Relations*, edited by Dania Koleilat Khatib, 123–44, Perspectives on Development in the Middle East and North Africa (MENA) Region, Singapore: Springer, 2021, https://doi.org/10.1007/978-981-15-5050-8_8.

CHAPTER FOUR

THE RISE OF FAR-RIGHT NATIONALISM, POPULISM, AND ISLAMOPHOBIA

In the last two decades, the political structure of many countries around the world has been challenged by new as well as revived ideological and political movements, which have also challenged the international system. Initially, these movements seemed to be more impactful on domestic political dynamics; however, they soon started reshaping foreign policy considerations. These movements had been present in Western societies for decades, but at the turn of the 21st century they came out of dormancy and produced new political forces. The reaction to the 9/11 terrorist attacks, the tenor of the clash of civilizations discourse in Western politics, the emergence of new international terror groups, and the 2008 financial meltdown and its sociological aftershocks contributed to the rise of far-right, populist, and Islamophobic groups in the West.

In country after country, these movements started to organize political groups and parties to challenge not only existing governments but also perceptions of state-society relations. Their rise sought to refashion intercommunal relations within nations in a way that threatened democratic norms and institutions. They utilized pre-existing discriminatory discourses and rhetoric against refugees, foreigners, and Muslims within their communities and benefited from the proliferation of new forms of social media. They have presented refugees and Muslims as an existential threat to the culture, identity, and well-being of their societies and nations. Building upon their similar rhetoric against Muslims and refugees, they established transnational cooperation and coordination with similar groups in other countries.

These reactionary movements share a pervading skepticism about globalization, international coalitions, and the growing emphasis on multiculturalism. The adherents of these movements do not only object to multiculturalism, but are also skeptical about anything foreign being allowed into their country. Social diversity is seen as a threat, which is not a particularly new phenomenon in many Western societies. What is relatively new with increasing globalization is that these sentiments typically come from groups who claim they have been marginalized or aggrieved by elite attitudes about cosmopolitanism, diversity, and inclusion. Their attitudes about their respective societies and their governments' international engagements do not fit well into the mainstream political spectrum.

Within the first two decades of the new millennium, these groups gathered support and often spread unsubstantiated and unverified information about refugees, Muslims, and foreigners. Their campaigns focused on fear as a coalescing dynamic in their messaging, which became an active part of the political discourse. What has changed in the last few years is not only the potency of such movements but also their increasing visibility in the public space[1] even to the extent that their discourse has been embraced by some mainstream politicians. This has extended to the rhetoric of policymakers, as far-right politicians have popularized their message among the masses, generating a top-down impact of far-right positions.[2] Around the world, these movements have risen for various purposes including serving specific ideologies or scapegoating certain groups for specific problems in a country.

Although these movements are considered as significant threat to intercommunal relations within societies and interstate relations in a region, political leaders shy away from taking strong positions against them. Especially due to the high degree of polarization across the political spectrum in Western countries, these groups started to be considered key actors in establishing winning and governing coalitions. More dangerously, the discourse and rhetoric of these groups started to be adopted by mainstream political parties and leaders to appeal to their sympathizers. This tactical move by mainstream parties normalized these marginalized discourses within the political spectrum. Thus, these fringe positions started to be embraced by voters of mainstream parties as well. These movements have evolved and become so influential trends in national politics that they have essentially become a normalized part of the latter. As President Erdoğan emphasizes, these currents can no longer be considered political as but they are driven by hatred, and in particular hatred of Islam and Muslims.[3]

In a rather short period of time, their discourse started to impact the foreign policy arena as well. The real problem was many analysts around the world considered this phenomenon an unavoidable wave of nationalism and disregarded any solutions to prevent its spread to other countries. Only a few nations, including Türkiye, took steps to stop this very dangerous far-right ideology. Despite hosting millions of refugees and suffering from the economic impact of large refugee inflows, President Erdoğan resisted any discourse and rhetoric that would cause policy changes targeting vulnerable populations. Just like other countries across Europe, some opportunistic politicians have tried to spread anti-refugee sentiment, but the Turkish public has been adequately aware of the necessity to resist such a wave in Türkiye. President Erdoğan, cognizant of the anti-refugee and anti-Islam movements across the world, called on the international community to resist and establish solidarity against these movements.

Islamophobia: The Cancer of the 21st Century

Islamophobia has been present in different parts of the world for decades. Just as with anti-Semitism, the Islamophobic ideology has spread steadily, propelled by persistent stereotypes about Muslims and preconceived notions about Islam.[4] In the 1980s, scholars such as Edward Said raised the issue of problematic coverage of Islam in Western media, which often associated the religion and its believers with political violence and terrorism.[5] This was also prevalent in Western popular culture, in which Muslims were portrayed as violent characters such as terrorists or criminals.[6] In the 1990s, the Huntingtonian concept of clash of civilizations circulated widely among Western scholars and policymakers. According to this discourse, Muslims and the Islamic world were presented as "other" to the Western civilization. In addition to being a security threat, Muslims and the Islamic world were presented as civilizational and cultural threats to the Western world. Supporters of this argument claimed that there would be an inevitable clash between Western civilization and the Islamic world. These trends of Islamophobia became more influential in the domestic and foreign policies of many countries following the 9/11 attacks, thereby changing the geopolitical landscape around the world.[7]

Although the Bush administration offered a message of unity in the immediate aftermath of the attacks by promising to clarify the essential separation between believers of Islam and terrorists, the existential sentiments of linking Muslims to terrorism amplified anti-Muslim sentiment within many segments of American society. As a result, there was a sharp rise in attacks against Muslim residents in the U.S. following 9/11. According to the FBI, religious-based hate crimes against Muslims after 9/11 rose 17 times above the numbers before the attacks of September 11.[8] At the same time, cases of discrimination against Muslims also became more frequent.[9]

Although Muslim-populated countries, such as Türkiye, were quick to express support for the U.S. against terrorists, this fact was not acknowledged and highlighted. The far-right media in the U.S. carelessly misinformed the public with reports that Muslims elsewhere celebrated the 9/11 attacks. This claim was repeated more than 15 years later by former president Trump, who said that Muslims in New Jersey celebrated the collapse of the World Trade Center and claimed that he witnessed such a display. None of the raw media footage, however, showed any evidence to back this claim and New Jersey law enforcement officials also could not corroborate it. Nevertheless, the claim spread among far-right segments of social media users and media outlets while being repeated frequently by ultra-conservative commentators.[10] The ease with which these claims spread and the willingness of some segments of American society to believe these claims demonstrated the potency of deep-seated skepticism and suspicion about Muslims.

Within the decade after the 9/11 attacks, the impact of these anti-Muslim feelings on society and politics in Western countries became evident, thereby eroding values and principles that had been articulated and developed since the latter part of the 20th century. Politicians in Europe and the United States discussed profiling the Muslim population while far-right groups presented Muslims as a threat to Western civilization.[11] Instead of focusing on fighting against international terrorism in its entirety, these groups leveraged their position from a cultural relativist perspective.[12] According to far-right groups, many Western nations enacted precautions to contain early signs of an "Islamic threat" against the security of their citizens, but this was not sufficient. They saw Islam and Muslims as a significant cultural threat that would undo the Western way of life. This threat potentially was more dangerous and existential than the threat of terrorism from radical groups. The far-right nationalists and populists wanted a culture war and Muslims were going to be at the receiving end of it.

Since then, there have been several effects connected to the rise of an anti-Muslim attitude. First, the number of hate crimes committed against Muslims has increased.[13] Whenever a terrorist incident occurs, anti-Muslim hate crimes in various cities in Western Europe and the U.S. spike in numbers.[14] For instance, one report shows that four weeks after the Paris terrorist attacks in 2015, there were some 45 anti-Muslim hate crimes committed in the U.S.[15] with individuals, Islamic community centers, and mosques as the main targets. Despite law enforcement investigations, policymakers in Europe and the U.S. have not actively managed public opinion to prevent the rising trend of Islamophobia.[16] Second, far-right politicians and groups have treated Muslims as "usual suspects," notably after the rise of DAESH and its terrorist attacks in Western countries.[17] Instead of neutralizing the roots of terrorism and arranging effective international cooperation that could curb the recruitment, financing, and transport of terrorists, many countries have rushed to scapegoating.[18] For many state leaders, this was an easier, convenient route given the urgency demanded in curbing and responding to terrorist attacks.

Profiling Muslim travelers has become a frequently used strategy. News outlets report frequent cases of Muslim travelers being abused or discriminated against by transportation security agents and border control authorities. Muslims have described this act of discrimination as "traveling while Muslim."[19] Some human rights organizations in Western countries have advocated for countries to reverse these policies, but government officials remain complicit, thereby signaling their approval of such restrictive measures.[20] Institutions of internal security publicly express their denial that such measures are being deployed, but independent investigations have proven otherwise.[21] Meanwhile, certain politicians in the West have continued to argue for even stricter control of Muslims in their countries.[22] This has extended to domestic surveillance measures against Muslims and their civil society organizations.[23]

In this second wave of discriminatory policies, it became common for candidates seeking office to expand the threshold for justifying Islamophobia. The conceptualization of Muslims as a threat to the well-being of society has seeped deeper into public discussions, as conservative politicians have offered their solutions "to deal with this problem" with every recommendation more restrictive and discriminatory.[24] In the 2016 presidential campaign, then candidate Trump magnified the tone when he suggested banning Muslims from entering the United States. After becoming president, he put into motion his version of a "Muslim Ban."[25]

The waves of Islamophobia reached Europe, especially within the context of the recent refugee crises emanating from Syria, Iraq, and Afghanistan. Ideological positions have overlapped among anti-immigration and anti-Muslim groups across the continent.[26] During and in the immediate aftermath of the refugee flows to Europe from conflict zones in the Middle East and North Africa, a major wave of anti-refugee/anti-Muslim sentiment spread just as rapidly. Terror attacks in major cities of Germany, Britain, France, and Spain led to the rapid rise of these sentiments. Studies on the perception of Muslims in Europe have demonstrated that a large group of Europeans consider Muslims as a threat. In one such survey, almost 50 percent of respondents in Germany and Switzerland considered Islam a threat.[27]

Anti-immigration groups have processed the anti-Muslim messages in presenting refugees as not only an economic and security threat to the European people, but also as an existential threat to the cultural integrity of Western nations[28] and the acknowledged "way of life" in European countries.[29] This "cultural threat" perception was partly responsible for the attempts of some European governments to enact legislation to restrict the religious freedom of Muslims.[30] Studies about the relationship between Islam and the West have indicated that 60 percent of survey respondents in France and Spain believe that Islam is incompatible with the West. The same study showed that this perception of Islam also influenced the perception of Muslims more broadly. Accordingly, nearly one-third of the respondents in Austria said that they do not want to have a Muslim neighbor.[31] Official reports by the Organization of Security and Cooperation in Europe and Europol have also highlighted the intensified negative attitudes and incidents of hate crimes against Muslims in Western countries.[32]

The rise of anti-refugee and anti-Muslim sentiments has been instrumental in the electoral success of far-right politicians who use fear to propel anti-refugee political platforms in order to build their voting base.[33] Unfortunately, Islamophobia has become more common in virtually every European country, as politicians have waged successful campaigns urging voters to be more vigilant about threats they claim arise from Islam and the presence of Muslims.[34] Even if some politicians were not elected, they continue to press the case by urging their constituencies to press legislators on anti-Muslim legislation that could extend to suppressing the right of religious freedom specifically for Muslims.[35] In one Pew Research report, it was argued that Europe experienced the largest increase in enacting restrictions for Muslims. The report demonstrated that regarding religious restrictions enacted by the government, Europe's score doubled over a 10-year period, as most of them affected Muslims, even if they were couched in language that was applicable to other confessional communities as well.[36]

Some countries have banned "wearing religious symbols or religious clothing, either completely or in certain circumstances (such as at public service jobs or photographs for official documents)."[37] The French government's decision to outlaw full face coverings was among the first steps which was followed by more substantial limitations on religious freedoms.[38] Later, the French government sought stricter measures in order to win popular support.[39] Other governments acted similarly against the religious freedom of Muslims. These forms of legislation and resolutions did not generate a strong reaction across Europe. Every inaction in the face of these resolutions encouraged far-right politicians in other countries to take similar measures and to make it harder for Muslims and refugees to live in that country.

The rise of Islamophobia is not only a problem in Europe and Western nations. Similar attitudes started to rise and intensify within the last two decades in different parts of the world as well. In some instances, however, these non-Western instances of Islamophobia are not receiving sufficient attention. Within the last two decades, bottom-up as well as government-sponsored sources of anti-Muslim attitudes and feelings have popped up with accelerated frequency in Asian countries. Although there are decades-old problems with Muslim minorities in these countries, governments started to take advantage of the global rise of Islamophobia by further suppressing the religious and political liberties of Muslim groups.

In countries, such as India, existing anti-Muslim attitudes have intensified, as evidenced by the Kashmir siege.[40] The Indian government proposed new citizenship laws, which were met with protests by the

Muslim population, and the government responded by cracking down on the protesters.[41] In Myanmar, vigilante groups together with the Myanmar army attacked communities of Muslim Rohingya people. Their attempt to ethnically cleanse the Muslim minority generated a major refugee crisis in Bangladesh.[42] In these countries, the "Islamic threat" discourse spread just as swiftly as it has in Western and European countries. Muslims have started to be considered as the "usual suspects" and have been marginalized within these countries.

The language of this Islamophobic and anti-refugee attitude carried over into foreign policy discussions as well. The Muslim ban in the United States produced a major diplomatic crisis between the U.S. and eight predominantly Muslim-populated countries.[43] The increasing anti-Muslim sentiment in the U.S. also affected the nation's global image, exacerbating already existing anti-Americanism. State-sponsored Islamophobia in France led to a crisis between France and Muslim countries. This was most apparent after France conducted dozens of raids and closed Muslim aid groups following the killing of a French schoolteacher by an extremist. President Macron's statements following the incident were considered offensive by Muslim countries and some carried out demonstrations against France. The governments of some Muslim countries reacted strongly against Macron's position against Islam. President Erdoğan of Türkiye and Prime Minister Imran Khan of Pakistan publicly criticized Macron's position.[44]

Waves of anti-Muslim and Islamophobic discourse developed in tandem with other radical movements across Western countries. Especially following the 2008 global financial crisis, far-right groups garnered support for their xenophobic positions and attitudes. While many finance and economics experts and officials focused on how to stop and reverse the 2008 economic meltdown, they failed to understand and act against the social aftershocks of the economic crisis. One of the most significant economic and social consequences of the 2008 economic crisis was rising unemployment across the world. The unemployment rates helped foment an audience that was receptive to xenophobic arguments through the scapegoating of immigrants and refugees as the culprits of the economic problems.[45]

In Germany, which is considered a special case because of its 20th-century history, a far-right, racist, and xenophobic movement achieved the status of the third-largest party in the 2017 elections.[46] This outcome surprised many observers of far-right politics, as Germany was considered an exception in Europe where the society is acutely cognizant of the potential threat of far-right groups.[47] The party brought together Islamophobic, xenophobic, and anti-immigrant slogans during its campaign, a common characteristic of far-right parties in other countries, including Le Pen's National Rally party in France. Targeting voters in the lower economic classes, these parties effectively inflamed feelings of anti-immigrant anxiety by presenting the potential threats these immigrants and refugees could pose to their livelihoods. More critically, the research demonstrated that refugees and immigrants were being framed negatively as Muslims by these groups for political gain, where they have attempted to render xenophobia and Islamophobia virtually inseparable from each other.[48]

The far-right groups in Europe, adopting an aggressive anti-immigrant platform, played a greater role in the politics and issues of the European Union. The most prominent example was the Brexit referendum, which led to the UK's exit from the European Union, due in part to the anti-refugee rhetoric. This rhetoric emboldened Islamophobic and xenophobic movements, and provoked concerns about the presence of Syrian refugees.[49] Fear-driven arguments elsewhere were joined with skepticism about international alliances, which, in turn, reinforced isolationist sentiment. These groups used the media efficiently to communicate such concerns and fear to the public, relying on inaccurate information, which was rarely challenged. Using social media platforms, these groups also deployed tactics of street politics, demonstrations, and attacks against refugees and immigrants.[50] They even targeted immigrants who had already been settled in the country for a long time and were earning their livelihoods. When it comes to attacking everything that is foreign and different, far-right and xenophobic groups do not differentiate between newcomer refugees and second or third-generation migrants living in their countries. As a result of this "effective campaigning," they managed to convince most of the voters to support Britain's exit from the European Union.

More worrisome were the major security risks these groups triggered through acts of extremism (e.g., hate crimes targeting individuals or small groups) and domestic terrorism (e.g., coordinated attacks on active, more densely populated gathering spots). On July 22, 2011, for example, Norway experienced the worst terrorist act in its history when Anders Behring Breivik killed eight people by detonating a car bomb in Oslo's government building district before shooting and killing 69 participants of a Workers' Youth League (AUF) summer camp on the island of Utøya. In his diaries, social media posts, and later in court, Breivik emphasized the threat that refugees posed to Western civilizations by considering the "Islamization of Europe" a major threat to European countries and their cultural legacy and security. He said, "We know that once the Muslims reach approximately 50 percent of the population there will be a conflict which is likely to result in enormous human suffering."[51] The conspiracy theories that Breivik wrote in his diaries would be shared and distributed by other far-right extremists elsewhere. Breivik postulated that Muslims represented the "demographic Jihad" by arguing that Muslims are intentionally increasing their population in Europe as part of a strategy to eventually replace Christians on the continent. According to Breivik, Muslims were making progress on this goal through "uncontrolled migration and uncontrolled breeding." Breivik argued that after reaching a certain threshold, Muslims in Europe will start killing their neighbors, namely Christians. Breivik imagined this as a pattern that would spread across Europe. After providing unverified statistics about demographic changes in Europe, he argued that European women have already been bullied, robbed, and even rapped by Muslims.[52] Breivik's discourse resembled the Huntingtonian concept of the clash of civilizations. He punctuated his writing with references to Christian teachings and the Bible to legitimize the violence he called for and to motivate and mobilize others to accept and follow through on his arguments.[53] Just as in the clash of civilizations argument, he contended that a global confrontation between Muslims and Christians is inevitable and unavoidable. Although his conspiracy theories had some followers and there were many in Europe who believed in such reports, the governments across Europe did not pay sufficient attention to the threat of these groups. In a few years, however, these conspiracy theories started to spread like wildfire and became a rallying cry for far-right political parties.

In 2019, a similar terrorist attack occurred in New Zealand at a mosque in Christchurch, killing more than 50 people. The profile of the terrorist in New Zealand was not much different than Breivik 's profile. In his social media posts and diaries, the perpetrator, Brenton Harrison Tarrant, referenced Breivik's arguments by mentioning the threat of refugees to European culture and civilization. The manifesto he posted online was titled "Great Replacement," a slogan that resonated among anti-immigrant groups in Europe. He wrote, "European peoples are dying out and being 'replaced' by immigrants with a different, inferior and dangerous culture."[54] The manifesto also mentioned a demographic and cultural decline in European countries due to the ongoing migration of Muslims. Once again, a domestic terrorist associated the low birth rates among white people and the trope of the so-called mass immigration of Muslims, and proclaimed the two as dangers to Europeans. Tarrant added that these circumstances generated economic problems for the predominant white race and threatened the economic well-being and social status of Europeans.[55] He argued that this would result in a "white genocide," the extermination of the white race, carried out by Muslims. Just as with Breivik, Tarrant also described Islam as a violent religion and depicted Muslim immigrants and refugees as rapists, attempting to legitimize the violence that he planned to exact on Muslims.[56] Tarrant also targeted Türkiye as a significant threat to Europe. He repeated the arguments of the clash of civilizations discourse, which became a foundation for many far-right extremists as they pressured their respective governments to adopt their positions and revise their policies on international relations. Tarrant's manifesto demonstrated the transnational nature of far-right terrorism and extremism.

The far right's assertiveness sought a similar "us versus them" approach to foreign policy, as it advocated in domestic policy circles. As previously mentioned, "others" can be interpreted rather widely to include different countries and international organizations. Thus, any form of international engagement generates suspicion and is considered questionable by these groups who promulgate the rise of "nation first" movements. While Trump's "America First" movement became the most significant symbol of this attitude in foreign policy, far-right movements elsewhere shared the American ideology. Their approaches followed similar tenets. These groups believe that the international system and other states pose a major threat to the existence and well-being of their nations. To protect the nation from these threats, these groups must inform the public about the dangers of globalization and how it hampers national interests. The elites who pursue globalism rather than national interests act as foreign agents who do not have their respective nation's interests in mind. According to them, a win-win situation in international relations is inconceivable. They believe international relations is a zero-sum game and whenever policymakers attempt to engage in international endeavors, they should approach such measures with caution and consider the merits of a "nation first" approach. Although many around the world have acknowledged that global problems necessitate the close cooperation and coordination of states, for far-right groups, issues such as climate change and pandemics should not be prioritized over national problems. Such groups prefer a selective isolationism in their approaches to global affairs. Any form of humanitarian intervention or international engagement to end human suffering in a crisis must be considered unacceptable in a nation's foreign policy - this is a position that has become dominant over the last two decades as many countries have shied away from pursuing humanitarian endeavors as essential foreign policy initiatives.

The "nation first" approach emphasizes unilateralism without the necessity of seeking guidance or input from international institutions for protecting national interests. Consultation with allies or trying to find a collective solution to the issues are not ideal solutions, far-right groups contend. Accordingly, multilateral settings are time consuming and unnecessarily prolong efforts to protect national interests. The skepticism is so potent that it becomes ever more difficult to achieve sustainable cooperation among nations. For these groups, cooperation in international affairs is only possible when other nations jump on the bandwagon of ensuring their respective nation's interests first before pursuing international engagement. The reality, though, is that their approach is impractical given how intertwined the destinies of nations have become on issues of common human impact (i.e., climate change and pandemics). The far-right expressions of Islamophobia and unconditional isolationist perspectives have done their part in destabilizing the geopolitical landscape and international institutions.

Despite the growing presence of these movements along with assertive and aggressive messages, few observers have tried to comprehend the long-term ramifications of an anti-internationalist discourse. Türkiye has warned that this must be addressed, especially as many xenophobic and Islamophobic movements in Europe have followed an anti-Türkiye position since their inception. Türkiye and Turks in Europe have been presented as the other by these groups. First, for many anti-immigrant groups, the Turkish diaspora constitutes the biggest threat to the traditional demographic profile of European countries, with German far-right groups as an example of those who have held this sentiment for a long time against Turkish immigrants. Meanwhile, European governments have ignored these dynamics. Far-right extremists in Germany voice conspiracy theories to build fear in their communities by claiming immigration would be difficult to control or halt if Türkiye joined the EU or if German officials liberalized their visa rules. Furthermore, the success of Turkish immigrants in Germany and their visibility in public spaces have been perceived as significant threats to the status of nativists in Germany.

Far-right groups would prefer that Turks remain second-class citizens. As a result, Turkish community centers and Turkish citizens have become the target of hate crimes not just in Germany but elsewhere on the continent. Far-right groups have argued for excluding Türkiye from the European Union, pushing tactics to make it impossible for Türkiye to develop friendly relations with other European nations. The real challenge has been that some politicians and governments have caved to the political demands of these groups. By adopting policies to appease the far-right extremist rhetoric, Western governments not only hurt their relations with Türkiye but have also given these groups leverage to influence foreign policy. Furthermore, this appeasement policy has also endangered the future of the European Union and the cultivation of diversity and multiculturalism in the Western world.

Continuing an exclusionary policy in the EU could legitimize far-right movements despite earnest calls from observers that governments in Europe and Western countries should dissuade citizens and policymakers from allowing the domestic policy concerns of political opportunists to promulgate isolationism as the only consideration for formulating foreign policy. The Turkish government has been vocal in expressing its discontent with this anti-Turkish discourse in European countries. Discrimination against immigrants with Turkish origins not only violates the rights of Turkish immigrants in these countries but also makes the integration process more difficult for these immigrants. President Erdoğan during his meetings with members of the Turkish diaspora in these countries always asserts that Turks should be integrated into the host communities but should avoid being assimilated. Furthermore, President Erdoğan has always warned the governments of host countries that a wave of anti-immigrant and anti-Turkish attitude in these countries can pave the way for increasing xenophobia, which could significantly endanger the peace and harmony within these societies.

Today, the anti-Türkiye attitude among far-right groups in Europe overlaps with the anti-refugee position of these groups. Türkiye has started to represent not only the origin of a group of immigrants in their countries but also the transfer point for refugees from Syria and other conflict zones. The Turkish government in numerous instances has asserted that the international community needs to take more responsibility in alleviating the refugee problem and governments should take strong positions instead of caving to far-right groups. The discriminatory and xenophobic discourse and demands of the far-right groups will have no limit in the future. Appeasing their demands will lead to further requests from these groups to discriminate against foreigners in their countries.

In Türkiye, there are also far-right groups, but these groups have remained a marginal element in Turkish society, unlike in many other countries. In Türkiye, public opinion appears to dovetail with the government's stance, despite attempts by several opposition parties to change the country's position on accepting refugees. Ankara was disinterested in seeking any significant appeasement of anti-refugee politicians and their movements. With public opinion consolidated behind the government's position, most opposition figures demurred from taking an aggressive anti-refugee stance. Second, the government has ensured that the public has received plenty of information about the arrival of refugees and how they are being processed and settled in Türkiye. The public has understood the refugee plight.

Thus, Türkiye has demonstrated that the anti-refugee wave of public resentment is not impossible to curb. It has also shown that humanitarian tragedies can be alleviated when there is a determined and committed government that aims to prevent humanitarian disasters not just in the affected region but elsewhere in the world. The current humanitarian disasters serve to emphasize a point that the international order cannot function or be legitimate if it is insensitive to human suffering. It is impractical to strengthen, stabilize, and reform an international order if nation-states easily subscribe to the demands of anti-refugee groups and political parties without considering the long-term implications of following such policies. Humanitarian disasters can exacerbate the pace of destabilizing a region while cementing dysfunctional environments, and fomenting political extremism and distrust internally and externally. Economic downturns, terrorist attacks, or a pandemic cannot become facile excuses for countries and international organizations to ignore humanitarian disasters. Türkiye has shown the world that it is feasible, constructive, and efficient to deal with humanitarian crises with an emphasis on cultivating collaborative engagement. Türkiye's model is instructive, and its features can be translated and emulated by members of the international community.

Since the increasing rise of Islamophobia around the world, the Turkish government has also exposed the danger that this wave can pose to Muslim minorities and minorities from other religions in these countries. With the rapid rise of Islamophobia, President Erdoğan has led efforts to contravene language that denigrates Islam and its believers. The Turkish government has warned the international community about the potentially negative outcomes of allowing hate discourse. Echoing the historical lessons of the Holocaust, the Turkish government has reminded European countries that this hate language could lead to a dangerous outcome. But European states have ignored the threat to their Muslim citizens and have not taken meaningful action to curb it. While some politicians and their respective movements have embraced Islamophobic discourse, it was Türkiye that responded to the smear campaigns against Islam.

Because of inaction, the world has seen violent attacks against Muslims across the world occur more frequently. For example, a Pew Research report in 2017 indicated that the number of assaults against Muslims in 2016 was the highest in 15 years. The report also indicated that "half of U.S. Muslim adults (50%) say that in recent years it has become more difficult to be a Muslim in the U.S., with 10% of this group attributing this to discrimination, racism and prejudice."[57] In Europe, an analysis of religious freedom challenges in France, the UK, Germany, the Netherlands, and Sweden concluded that "anti-Muslim discrimination is somewhat pervasive in all aspects of the employment process; includes increased acts and threats of violence that disproportionately impacts women; and is manifest in opposition to mosque construction projects."[58] Türkiye has offered to cooperate with European states, which it hoped would lead to a unified and productive response to smear campaigns targeting Muslims and Islam. Unfortunately, this request has also been ignored. As a sponsor of the Alliance of Civilizations Initiative, Türkiye aims to fight against Islamophobia. President Erdoğan has stated that it is a duty for every civilized nation around the world to fight against the hate language that targets Muslims. He believes that the tragedies in Myanmar are a showcase of what this language can generate in the future in different countries. President Erdoğan has raised this issue in almost every international forum in the last several years. Especially during the UN General Assembly meetings, President Erdoğan has asked leaders around the world to unite against this extremely dangerous political discourse. Islamophobia does not only endanger the Muslims in non-Muslim majority countries, but also threatens to destabilize the entire international system.

ENDNOTES

1 Mudde, Cas, "Nativism Is Driving the Far-Right Surge in Europe – and It Is Here to Stay," *The Guardian*, November 12, 2019, http://www.theguardian.com/global/commentisfree/2019/nov/12/nativism-is-driving-the-far-right-surge-in-europe-and-it-is-here-to-stay.

2 "France's Election Season Kicks off with Le Pen Sparring on Islam," Bloomberg, February 11, 2021, https://www.bloomberg.com/news/articles/2021-02-11/france-s-election-season-kicks-off-with-le-pen-sparring-on-islam.

3 Recep Tayyip, *A Fairer World Is Possible: A Proposed Model for United Nations Reform*, Istanbul, September 2021, p. 99.

4 Devji, Faisal, "From Xinjiang to Germany: How Did Islamophobia Become a Global Phenomenon?" *The Guardian*, March 27, 2020, http://www.theguardian.com/commentisfree/2020/mar/27/xinjiang-germany-islamophobia-global-phenomenon.

5 Said, Edward W, *Covering Islam: How the Media and the Experts Determine How We See the Rest of the World*, Revised edition, New York: Vintage, 1997.

6 Emami, Gazelle, "24 Is Back to Make You Fear Muslim Terrorists Again," Vulture, n.d., accessed August 10, 2021. https://www.vulture.com/2017/02/24-legacy-muslim-terrorists-terrible-timing.html.

7 Dubosh, Emily, Mixalis Poulakis, and Nour Abdelghani, "Islamophobia and Law Enforcement in a Post 9/11 World," *Islamophobia Studies Journal* 3 (1): 138–57, 2015, https://doi.org/10.13169/islastudj.3.1.0138.

8 "Statistics," n.d., https://www.mpac.org/programs/hate-crime-prevention/statistics.php.

9 Ibid.

10 Kessler, Glenn, "Analysis | Trump's Outrageous Claim That 'Thousands' of New Jersey Muslims Celebrated the 9/11 Attacks," *The Washington Post*, November 22, 2015, https://www.washingtonpost.com/news/fact-checker/wp/2015/11/22/donald-trumps-outrageous-claim-that-thousands-of-new-jersey-muslims-celebrated-the-911-attacks/.

11 Lenz-Raymann, Kathrin, "*Securitization of Islam: A Vicious Circle*: Counter-Terrorism and Freedom of Religion in Central Asia" in Securitization of Islam: A Vicious Circle, 1–4, Counter-Terrorism and Freedom of Religion in Central Asia, Transcript Verlag, 2014, https://www.jstor.org/stable/j.ctv1fxgjp.1.

12 "Islamophobia: Understanding Anti-Muslim Sentiment in the West," Gallup.com, December 12, 2011, https://news.gallup.com/poll/157082/islamophobia-understanding-anti-muslim-sentiment-west.aspx.

13 Frazee, Gretchen, "What the New Zealand Shootings Tell Us about the Rise in Hate Crimes," PBS NewsHour, March 15, 2019, https://www.pbs.org/newshour/world/what-the-new-zealand-shootings-tell-us-about-the-rise-in-hate-crimes.

14 Wilson, Chris, and Sanjal Shastri, "Hate Crimes against Muslims Spiked after the Mosque Attacks, and Ardern Promises to Make Such Abuse Illegal," The Conversation, n.d., http://theconversation.com/hate-crimes-against-muslims-spiked-after-the-mosque-attacks-and-ardern-promises-to-make-such-abuse-illegal-147347.

15 Levin, Brian, "Explaining the Rise in Hate Crimes against Muslims in the US," The Conversation, n.d., accessed http://theconversation.com/explaining-the-rise-in-hate-crimes-against-muslims-in-the-us-80304.

16 Misra, Tanvi, "Anti-Muslim Incidents in America, Mapped," Bloomberg, March 9, 2018, https://www.bloomberg.com/news/articles/2018-03-09/anti-muslim-incidents-are-increasing-across-america.

17 Forde, Kaelyn, "DAESH Counting on Anti-Muslim Backlash 'to Sharpen the Divide,' Experts Warn," ABC News, June 7, 2017, https://abcnews.go.com/International/isis-counting-anti-muslim-backlash-sharpen-divide-experts/story?id=47862508.

18 Martin, Michel and Arsalan Ifitkhar, "Muslims Are Just the Latest in History of Scapegoats, Author Says," *NPR*, June 5, 2016, sec. Author Interviews, https://www.npr.org/2016/06/05/480861394/muslims-are-just-the-latest-in-history-of-scapegoats-author-says.

19 Khaleeli, Homa, "The Perils of 'Flying While Muslim,'" *The Guardian*, August 8, 2016, http://www.theguardian.com/world/2016/aug/08/the-perils-of-flying-while-muslim.

20 Luongo, Michael T, "Traveling While Muslim Complicates Air Travel," *The New York Times*, November 7, 2016, sec. Business, https://www.nytimes.com/2016/11/08/business/traveling-while-muslim-complicates-air-travel.html.

21 Ackerman, Spencer, "TSA Screening Program Risks Racial Profiling amid Shaky Science – Study," *The Guardian*, February 8, 2017, http://www.theguardian.com/us-news/2017/feb/08/tsa-screening-racial-religious-profiling-aclu-study.

22 Phillips, Amber, "Donald Trump Calls Profiling Muslims 'Common Sense,'" *The Washington Post*, June 19, 2016, https://www.washingtonpost.com/news/post-politics/wp/2016/06/19/donald-trump-calls-profiling-muslims-common-sense/.

23 Allyn, Bobby, "'We're Supposed to Do That': Bloomberg Defends NYPD's Spying of Muslims After 9/11," *NPR*, February 27, 2020, sec. Politics, https://www.npr.org/2020/02/27/810181314/we-re-supposed-to-do-that-bloomberg-defends-nypd-s-spying-of-muslims-after-9-11.

24 "Angela Merkel Endorses Burka Ban 'Wherever Legally Possible,'" BBC News, December 6, 2016, sec. Europe. https://www.bbc.com/news/world-europe-38226081.

25 "Timeline of the Muslim Ban," ACLU of Washington, May 23, 2017, https://www.aclu-wa.org/pages/timeline-muslim-ban.

26 Virchow, Fabian, "PEGIDA: Understanding the Emergence and Essence of Nativist Protest in Dresden," *Journal of Intercultural Studies* 37 (6): 541–55, 2016, https://doi.org/10.1080/07256868.2016.1235026.

27 El Menouar, Yasemin and Sasnal Patrycja, "There's a Social Pandemic Poisoning Europe: Hatred of Muslims | Patrycja Sasnal and Yasemin El Menouar," *The Guardian*, September 28, 2020, http://www.theguardian.com/commentisfree/2020/sep/28/europe-social-pandemic-hatred-muslims-blm.

28 Damhuis, Koen, "Why Dutch Populists Are Exceptional," Brookings (blog), November 30, https://www.brookings.edu/articles/why-dutch-populists-are-exceptional/.

29 Trilling, Daniel, "'Protecting the European Way of Life' from Migrants Is a Gift to the Far Right," *The Guardian*, September 13, 2019, http://www.theguardian.com/commentisfree/2019/sep/13/protecting-europe-migrants-far-right-eu-nationalism.

30 Müller, Marco, "Where Are 'Burqa Bans' in Europe?" Deutsche Welle, January 8, 2019, https://www.dw.com/en/where-are-burqa-bans-in-europe/a-49843292.

31 El Menouar and Sasnal, "There's a Social Pandemic Poisoning Europe: Hatred of Muslims."

32 "Security Concerns of Muslim Communities," n.d., https://www.osce.org/odihr/infographic-muslim-security-guide.

33 Pickel, Gert and Cemal Öztürk, "The Varying Challenge of Islamophobia for the EU: On Anti-Muslim Resentments and Its Dividend for Right-Wing Populists and Eurosceptics—Central and Eastern Europe in a Comparative Perspective" in *Illiberal Trends and Anti-EU Politics in East Central Europe*, edited by Astrid Lorenz and Lisa H. Anders, 57–80. Palgrave Studies in European Union Politics. Cham: Springer International Publishing, 2020. https://doi.org/10.1007/978-3-030-54674-8_3.

34 Massoumi, Narzanin, "Opinion | Why Is Europe So Islamophobic?" *The New York Times*, March 6, 2020, sec. Opinion, https://www.nytimes.com/2020/03/06/opinion/europe-islamophobia-attacks.html.

35 Mahmood, Basit, "Why Muslims Should Still Be Afraid of the Dutch Election Outcome, Even Though Wilders Lost," *The Independent*, March 16, 2017, https://www.independent.co.uk/voices/dutchelectiongeertwildersmarkruttenetherlandspopulismislam-a7632936.html.

36 "Europe Experienced a Surge in Government Restrictions on Religious Activity over the Last Decade," Pew Research Center (blog), n.d., https://www.pewresearch.org/fact-tank/2019/07/29/europe-experienced-a-surge-in-government-restrictions-on-religious-activity-over-the-last-decade/.

37 Ibid.

38 Picheta, Rob, "France's Niqab Ban Violates Human Rights, UN Committee Says," CNN, October 23, 2018, https://www.cnn.com/2018/10/23/europe/france-niqab-ban-un-intl/index.html.

39 McAuley, James. "Macron Outlines New Law to Prevent Islamic 'Separatism' in France," *The Washington Post*, n.d., accessed August 10, 2021, https://www.washingtonpost.com/world/europe/macron-islam-france/2020/10/02/ba8a1dcc-04bc-11eb-b92e-029676f9ebec_story.html.

40 Bhattacharya, Ananya, "The 550-Day 4G Blackout Cost Kashmir's Economy $4.2 Billion," Quartz, February 9, 2021, https://qz.com/india/1970363/the-550-day-4g-blackout-cost-kashmirs-economy-4-2-billion/.

41 "Citizenship Amendment Bill: India's New 'Anti-Muslim' Law Explained," BBC News, December 11, 2019, sec. India, https://www.bbc.com/news/world-asia-india-50670393.

42 Maizland, Lindsay and Eleanor Albert, "What Forces Are Fueling Myanmar's

Rohingya Crisis?" Council on Foreign Relations, January 23, 2020, https://www.cfr.org/backgrounder/rohingya-crisis.

43 "Donald Trump's Immigration Order Is Bad Foreign Policy | National News | US News," US News & World Report, January 30, 2017, //www.usnews.com/news/national-news/articles/2017-01-30/donald-trumps-immigration-order-is-bad-foreign-policy.

44 Erlanger, Steven, "Muslim Countries Denounce French Response to Killing of Teacher, Urge Boycott," *The New York Times*, October 27, 2020, sec. World, https://www.nytimes.com/2020/10/27/world/europe/French-Muslims-Turkey-crackdown.html.

45 "Perspective - 'There Is No Evidence That Migrants Steal Jobs,'" France 24, September 2, 2019, https://www.france24.com/en/20190902-perspective-jonathan-portes-economic-impact-migration-migrants-europe-unemployment.

46 Clarke, Seán, "German Elections 2017: Full Results," *The Guardian*, n.d., accessed August 10, 2021, https://www.theguardian.com/world/ng-interactive/2017/sep/24/german-elections-2017-latest-results-live-merkel-bundestag-afd.

47 Wildman, Sarah, "Meet the Far-Right Party That's Bringing Racism and Xenophobia Back to Germany," Vox, September 26, 2017, https://www.vox.com/world/2017/9/26/16360916/afd-german-far-right-racism-xenophobia.

48 Einbinder, Nicole, "How the Far Right Has Reshaped the Refugee Debate in Europe," Frontline, January 22, 2018, https://www.pbs.org/wgbh/frontline/article/how-the-far-right-has-reshaped-the-refugee-debate-in-europe/.

49 Hall, Richard, "How the Brexit Campaign Used Refugees to Scare Voters," The World from PRX, June 24, 2016, https://www.pri.org/stories/2016-06-24/how-brexit-campaign-used-refugees-scare-voters.

50 Ekman, Mattias, "Anti-Refugee Mobilization in Social Media: The Case of Soldiers of Odin," *Social Media + Society* 4 (1): 2056305118764431. 2018, https://doi.org/10.1177/2056305118764431.

51 Richards, Barry, "What Drove Anders Breivik?" *Contexts* 13 (4): 42–47, 2014, https://doi.org/10.1177/1536504214558216.

52 Brown, Andrew, "Anders Breivik Is Not Christian but Anti-Islam," *The Guardian*, July 24, 2011, http://www.theguardian.com/commentisfree/andrewbrown/2011/jul/24/norway-anders-behring-breivik-beliefs.

53 Strømmen, Hannah, "Christian Terror in Europe? The Bible in Anders Behring Breivik's Manifesto," *Journal of the Bible and Its Reception* 4 (1): 147–69, 2017, https://doi.org/10.1515/jbr-2017-2006.

54 "New Zealand Mosque Shooting: What Is Known about the Suspect?" BBC News, March 18, 2019, sec. Asia, https://www.bbc.com/news/world-asia-47579243.

55 Ibid.

56 Beutel, Alejandro, "The New Zealand Terrorist's Manifesto: A Look at Some of the Key Narratives, Beliefs and Tropes | START.Umd.Edu," April 30, 2019, https://www.start.umd.edu/news/new-zealand-terrorists-manifesto-look-some-key-narratives-beliefs-and-tropes.

57 Kishi, Katayoun, "Assaults against Muslims in U.S. Surpass 2001 Level," Pew Research Center (blog), November 15, 2017, https://www.pewresearch.org/fact-tank/2017/11/15/assaults-against-muslims-in-u-s-surpass-2001-level/.

58 Abdelkader, Engy, "A Comparative Analysis of European Islamophobia: France, UK, Germany, Netherlands, and Sweden," *UCLA Journal of Islamic and Near Eastern Law* 16 (1), https://doi.org/10.5070/N4161038735.

CONCLUSION

The world is in a constant state of crisis and the current international order is failing to facilitate or assure peace and stability. The more familiar challenges such as regional conflict, migration, and global inequities are being compounded by newer threats including cybercrimes, a competitive race to claim outer space as territory, climate change, environmental disasters, and infectious diseases. The compounding of global crises has become virtually unmanageable, and the international system is inadequate in its current form to respond on multiple fronts. The delay of an urgently needed reform of the international order potentially aggravates the likelihood and intensity of human peril. As the global balance of power has shifted, new centers of power have emerged. Türkiye is situated in one of the most logistically consequential parts of the world, at the cusp of two continents with enormous economic significance, especially in the flows of capital and services for billions of people. The same juncture is dominated by pressures of regional conflict, migration, and instability. For two decades now, Türkiye has been a prominent advocate of global cooperation and reform of the international order.

In this monograph, I have discussed the failures and shortcomings of the international system in addressing specific contemporary global challenges that reverberate from region to region. In tandem, I have documented Türkiye's clear propositions for improving the international order's efficacy and relevance. Türkiye's specific proposals have been outlined here so as to direct the discourse toward constructive engagement on resolving and reforming how institutions can respond to entrenched and emerging crises. Türkiye's perspectives have led to mature, carefully deliberated proposals, given that the country has been, directly or indirectly, affected at some point by the spectrum of global conflicts, waves of migration, and geopolitical instability. As a country whose national interests in a region can only be sustainably assured through peaceful and stabilizing initiatives, Türkiye will continue to contextualize crises and ongoing problems through multiple lenses of closing the equity gap; highlighting and reconciling double standards in policy approaches; and advocating for the relief and redress of injustices that are endemic to the current international order.

The discussion of the international order crisis highlights the severe consequences of an international system that more often reflects global power imbalances rather than the political will to coordinate and remedy them. The built-in structural power inequities in the institutions of the international system have been tolerated and perpetuated by those who have benefited the most from the system's status quo. But this has come with a huge cost for the world. Instead of prioritizing stability and peace at the modest expense of the national interests of the great powers, the international order appears to operate with the great powers' interests as sole priorities. From migration to climate change, regional conflicts to emerging 21st-century threats, the international community more often has acted only when the great powers were most concerned about the issues involved. And even then, the actions of the international community were driven by the interests of the powerful rather than those of the global community.

Some discussions and the conclusions provided in this book present, indeed, a bleak picture. But realistic diagnosis can lead to effective solutions, and it reinforces the possibilities we can be hopeful about. Türkiye and its current leadership are a good example, encouraging the global community not to wait for the great powers to lead the way in solutions. Türkiye is aware that no single country has the panacea to resolve the existing problems but it also believes that international cooperation is always possible. As noted repeatedly, the existing international mechanisms of cooperation are not only inadequate, but also tend to produce and worsen the crises.

In the midst of different crises in the world, despite the failures of the international community and its conventional institutions, Türkiye has developed a reputation as a major humanitarian actor. The country not only hosts millions of refugees, but also extends a hand to those in need within its region as well as those in countries farther away. In addition, Türkiye has advocated for a practical and candid conversation about the current state of affairs in terms of the international order along with the implications of power politics and how great power interests appear to supersede those of other nations and regions which are directly affected by nearby conflicts and hostilities. Türkiye's proactive involvement in regional crises by engaging all actors without demonizing, isolating, or preferring one over another is instructive. Türkiye's more flexible accommodations are worth considering against other efforts, often led by great powers, which have precluded meaningful negotiations and inhibited potential solutions. Türkiye also raises its concerns about existing and emerging inequalities in the world. It believes that without justice there will not be peace, stability, and prosperity across the world. It advocates for meaningful input by both developing nations and the least developed nations in order to fashion policies and tactics that address equity gaps.

Turkish President Erdoğan's consistent calls on world leaders to come to the table on global challenges and to establish coordination mechanisms have produced some results, but there is a lot more to be done. Countries tend to prioritize their narrow self-interests, but they must also seek ways to align their national interests with the broader goals of stability and peace. Türkiye has consistently tried to align its interests with regional stability and peace over the past two decades, and its approach has had an impact in resolving some crises. When one looks at crises in Somalia, Yemen, Libya, the Eastern Mediterranean, Syria, the Balkans, or the Caucasus, Türkiye regularly appears as a stability-seeking power advocating for dialogue and peace between parties. Türkiye also commits and engages in multilateral forums to bring about solutions with the understanding that only a multiplicity of stakeholders can provide true and lasting solutions.

Türkiye's rhetoric against socioeconomic inequities and cultural demonization has been rigorous, emphasizing that these are not just symptoms but also causes of the global challenges facing humanity.

For the world to become safer and more hospitable for future generations, the community of nations must strengthen the humanitarian and human-centered approach in reforming and restructuring international institutions. The centuries-old game of great power politics can no longer be the basis of a coordinated, collaborative, and cohesive international system. History has provided plenty of evidence of the negative consequences of designing an international order shaped heavily by the interests of the most powerful nations. The liberal international order, as such, consistently favors the powerful nations and fails the less privileged ones. As a nation hosting millions of refugees and with a human-centered foreign policy, Türkiye's experience can inform and enlighten others about the task of designing institutions and developing global cooperation mechanisms driven by the interests of the less powerful and the global community. Forging a new international order that is sensitive to inclusion and equity covering more than a handful of historically powerful nations may be the best and only option for handling the intricate web of crises that are more intertwined than ever before.

The challenges of our day are going to require multigenerational and multinational efforts at a scale not experienced before in human history. Global stability and peace should not be sacrificed to the narrowly defined self-interests of the most powerful nations. The international community and multilateral institutions must be reformed and rendered truly effective. Xenophobia and Islamophobia should no longer be tolerated in the face of the humanitarian crises of our age. Climate change must be addressed in a fair and equitable manner. While addressing the root causes of reactionary movements and global inequities, the world must cooperate to confront injustice around the world head-on. The Turkish experience under the leadership of President Erdoğan over the past two decades provides a powerful example for nations around the world to emulate. Türkiye under Erdoğan's leadership has shown the world that a responsible and sound leadership can make enormous contributions to regional peace and stability as well as global solutions.

Türkiye has behaved as a proactive participant of the international system while pointing out its shortcomings and failures in the process of providing solutions. From terrorism to climate change and geopolitical challenges to the COVID-19 pandemic, Türkiye has provided both criticism and solutions as a responsible and constructive actor in the international system. Türkiye has never shied away from stepping up to resolve crises in its region and making meaningful contributions to global challenges. Our planet is far from ready to confront the current and future challenges lurking ahead. The international community and institutions will almost certainly disappoint as we have seen during the COVID-19 pandemic. However, there are a lot of reasons to be hopeful especially when one looks at the example of countries like Türkiye, which truly cares about a sustainable future for not only Turkish people but all humanity. Other nations must follow this example to ensure a safe and secure future for our planet. A reformed and renewed international system is an absolute necessity and Türkiye is ready to contribute to its rebuilding. All nations must participate in this effort based on fair and equitable burden-sharing to address global challenges for a prosperous and peaceful future.

BIBLIOGRAPHY

Abdelkader, Engy, "A Comparative Analysis of European Islamophobia: France, UK, Germany, Netherlands, and Sweden," *UCLA Journal of Islamic and Near Eastern Law* 16 (1), https://doi.org/10.5070/N4161038735.

Abdulrazaq, Tallha and Gareth Stansfield, "The Enemy Within: DAESH and the Conquest of Mosul," *The Middle East Journal* 70 (4): 525–42, 2016, https://www.jstor.org/stable/26427457.

Ackerman, Spencer, "TSA Screening Program Risks Racial Profiling amid Shaky Science – Study," *The Guardian*, February 8, 2017, http://www.theguardian.com/us-news/2017/feb/08/tsa-screening-racial-religious-profiling-aclu-study.

Allah, Milad Alodet, "An Account of the 2008 Syrian–Israeli Negotiations in Turkey," *Contemporary Arab Affairs* 9 (1): 100–114, 2016, https://doi.org/10.1080/17550912.2015.1118208.

Allinson, Tom, "Libya: Turkish Strategy Leaves Haftar on the Defensive | DW | 07.05.2020," Deutsche Welle, July 5, 2020, https://www.dw.com/en/libya-turkish-strategy-leaves-haftar-on-the-defensive/a-53365043.

Allyn, Bobby, "'We're Supposed to Do That': Bloomberg Defends NYPD's Spying of Muslims After 9/11," *NPR*, February 27, 2020, sec. Politics, https://www.npr.org/2020/02/27/810181314/we-re-supposed-to-do-that-bloomberg-defends-nypd-s-spying-of-muslims-after-9-11.

Alsayed, Ghaith, and Sarah El Deeb, "Virus Threat 'A New Terror' in Syria's Scarred Idlib Region," AP NEWS, April 20, 2021, https://apnews.com/article/ap-top-news-civil-wars-coronavirus-pandemic-syria-fa6f5a2f0c2f80922239ff96b98600e4.

Altun, Fahrettin, "11 Eylül Literatürü ve Bizden Neden Nefret Ediyorlar Sorusu Üzerine," *Tezkire*, Year: 10, No: 25, March/April 2002.

Altunisik, Meliha and Esra Cuhadar, "Turkey's Search for a Third Party Role in Arab–Israeli Conflicts: A Neutral Facilitator or a Principal Power Mediator?"

Mediterranean Politics 15 (3): 371–92, 2010, https://doi.org/10.1080/13629395.2010.517101.

"Amid Worsening Conditions in Yemen, More Somali Refugees Opt to Return," UNHCR, May 31, 2019, https://www.unhcr.org/news/briefing/2019/5/5cf0e7eb4/amid-worsening-conditions-yemen-somali-refugees-opt-return.html.

Amnesty International, 2019, "Afghanistan's Refugees: Forty Years of Dispossession," n.d., https://www.amnesty.org/en/latest/news/2019/06/Afghanistan-refugees-forty-years/.

"Angela Merkel Endorses Burka Ban 'Wherever Legally Possible,'" BBC News, December 6, 2016, sec. Europe. https://www.bbc.com/news/world-europe-38226081.

"Annan to Meet with 'Group of Friends' of Iraq to Chart Way Forward," UN News, February 18, 2004, https://news.un.org/en/story/2004/02/94442-annan-meet-group-friends-iraq-chart-way-forward.

"Annual Report: Moldova 2013," Amnesty International USA, 2013, https://www.amnestyusa.org/reports/annual-report-moldova-2013/.

Arango, Tim, Anne Barnard, and Ceylan Yeginsu, "Turkey's Military Plunges into Syria, Enabling Rebels to Capture DAESH Stronghold," *The New York Times*, August 24, 2016, sec. World, https://www.nytimes.com/2016/08/25/world/middleeast/Turkey-syria-isis.html.

Babst, Stefanie, "The Coronavirus Pandemic Hits NATO: Five Potential Implications," April 14, 2020, https://www.europeanleadershipnetwork.org/commentary/the-coronavirus-pandemic-hits-nato-five-potential-implications/.

Bathke, Benjamin, "Austrian Chancellor Warns of New Refugee Flows, Says Deportations to Afghanistan Will Continue," InfoMigrants, July 26, 2021. https://www.infomigrants.net/en/post/33865/austrian-chancellor-warns-of-new-refugee-flows-says-deportations-to-Afghanistan-will-continue.

Beauchamp, Zack, "DAESH Captured and Executed James Foley and Steven Sotloff, Two American Journalists," Vox, November 20, 2018, https://www.vox.com/2018/11/20/17996042/isis-captured-and-executed-james-foley-and-steven-sotloff-two-american-journalists.

Beirens, Hanne, "Cracked Foundation, Uncertain Future: Structural Weaknesses in the Common European Asylum System," Migrationpolicy.Org, March 16, 2018, https://www.migrationpolicy.org/research/structural-weaknesses-common-european-asylum-system.

Bennhold, Katrin, "Leaders of Turkey and Israel Clash at Davos Panel," *The New York Times*, January 29, 2009, sec. World, https://www.nytimes.com/2009/01/30/world/europe/30clash.html.

Bennis, Phyllis, "The United Nations and Palestine: Partition and Its Aftermath," *Arab Studies Quarterly* 19 (3): 47–76, 1997.

Beutel, Alejandro, "The New Zealand Terrorist's Manifesto: A Look at Some of the Key Narratives, Beliefs and Tropes | START.Umd.Edu," April 30, 2019, https://www.start.umd.edu/news/new-zealand-terrorists-manifesto-look-some-key-narratives-beliefs-and-tropes.

Bhattacharya, Ananya, "The 550-Day 4G Blackout Cost Kashmir's Economy $4.2 Billion," Quartz, February 9, 2021, https://qz.com/india/1970363/the-550-day-4g-blackout-cost-kashmirs-economy-4-2-billion/.

Bilefsky, Dan, "17,000 Migrants Stranded in Croatia by Border Crackdown," *The New York Times*, September 18, 2015, sec. World, https://www.nytimes.com/2015/09/19/world/europe/refugee-migrant-crisis-europe.html.

Boykoff, Pamela, Clare Sebastian, and Valentina Di Donato, "In the Race to Secure Medical Supplies, Countries Ban or Restrict Exports," CNN, n.d., https://www.cnn.com/2020/03/27/business/medical-supplies-export-ban/index.html.

Brown, Andrew, "Anders Breivik Is Not Christian but Anti-Islam," *The Guardian*, July 24, 2011, http://www.theguardian.com/commentisfree/andrewbrown/2011/jul/24/norway-anders-behring-breivik-beliefs.

Brown, Cameron S., "Turkey in the Gulf Wars of 1991 and 2003," *Turkish Studies* 8 (1): 85–119, 2007, https://doi.org/10.1080/14683840601162054.

Brown, David, "'The War on Terrorism Would Not Be Possible without NATO': A Critique," *Contemporary Security Policy* 25 (3): 409-29, 2004, https://doi.org/10.1080/1352326042000330583.

Bruni, Frank, "Fears in Turkey That Its Cyprus Problem Is Alienating Europe," *The New York Times*, April 10, 2003, sec. World, https://www.nytimes.com/2003/04/10/world/fears-in-Turkey-that-its-cyprus-problem-is-alienating-europe.html.

Buckley, Caitlin Alyce, "Learning from Libya, Acting in Syria," *Journal of Strategic Security* 5 (2): 81–104, 2012.

Burr, William, "A Brief History of U.S.-Iranian Nuclear Negotiations," *Bulletin of the Atomic Scientists* 65 (1): 21–34, 2009, https://doi.org/10.2968/065001004.

Byman, Daniel, "An Autopsy of the Iraq Debacle: Policy Failure or Bridge Too Far?" *Security Studies* 17 (4): 599–643, 2008, https://doi.org/10.1080/09636410802507974.

Caporaso, James A, "Europe's Triple Crisis and the Uneven Role of Institutions: The Euro, Refugees and Brexit," *JCMS: Journal of Common Market Studies* 56 (6): 1345–61, 2018, https://doi.org/10.1111/jcms.12746.

CBS Evening News, Boats from Greece Confront Refugees at Sea with Guns, n.d., https://www.youtube.com/watch?v=7wo0pY63Om8.

Çelenk, Ayşe Aslihan, "The Restructuring of Turkey's Policy towards Cyprus: The Justice and Development Party's Struggle for Power," *Turkish Studies* 8 (3): 349–63, 2007, https://doi.org/10.1080/14683840701489092.

Çelik, Mehmet, "Turkey Faults NATO for Inactivity against US-Backed Terror Army on Syrian Border," *Daily Sabah*, January 17, 2018, https://www.dailysabah.com/diplomacy/2018/01/17/Turkey-faults-nato-for-inactivity-against-us-backed-terror-army-on-syrian-border.

Charap, Samuel, Elina Treyger, and Edward Geist, "Understanding Russia's Intervention in Syria," October 2019, https://www.rand.org/pubs/research_reports/RR3180.html.

"Citizenship Amendment Bill: India's New 'Anti-Muslim' Law Explained," BBC News, December 11, 2019, sec. India, https://www.bbc.com/news/world-asia-india-50670393.

Clarke, Seán, "German Elections 2017: Full Results," *The Guardian*, n.d., accessed August 10, 2021, https://www.theguardian.com/world/ng-interactive/2017/sep/24/german-elections-2017-latest-results-live-merkel-bundestag-afd.

Clayton, J, "UNHCR Chief Issues Key Guidelines for Dealing with Europe's

Refugee Crisis," UNHCR, September 4, 2015, https://www.unhcr.org/news/latest/2015/9/55e9793b6/unhcr-chief-issues-key-guidelines-dealing-europes-refugee-crisis.html.

Chazan, Guy, "Turkey Grants U.S. Right To Airspace for Iraq War," *The Wall Street Journal*, March 21, 2003, sec. News, https://www.wsj.com/articles/SB104817621392697092O.

Cohen, Dan, "Op-Ed: Why a PPE Shortage Still Plagues America and What We Need to Do about It," CNBC, August 22, 2020, https://www.cnbc.com/2020/08/22/coronavirus-why-a-ppe-shortage-still-plagues-the-us.html.

"Collective Defence - Article 5," NATO, n.d., accessed August 10, 2021. http://www.nato.int/cps/en/natohq/topics_110496.htm.

Connelly, Andrew, "Refugees Suffer PTSD and Attempt Suicide in Greece," The World from PRX, April 10, 2017, https://www.pri.org/stories/2017-04-10/refugees-suffer-ptsd-and-attempt-suicide-greece.

"Community, Work, and School," Centers for Disease Control and Prevention, February 11, 2020, https://www.cdc.gov/coronavirus/2019-ncov/community/health-equity/race-ethnicity.html.

"Coronavirus Response: Turkish Medical Aid Arrives in Spain and Italy," NATO, n.d., http://www.nato.int/cps/en/natohq/news_174826.htm.

"COVID-19 and the Least Developed Countries | Department of Economic and Social Affairs," 2020, May 1, 2020, https://www.un.org/development/desa/dpad/publication/un-desa-policy-brief-66-covid-19-and-the-least-developed-countries/.

"COVID-19 Threatens Refugee Camps," n.d., International Rescue Committee (IRC), https://www.rescue.org/covid-19-threatens-refugee-camps.

Crail, Peter, "Brazil, Turkey Broker Fuel Swap with Iran | Arms Control Association," 2021, https://www.armscontrol.org/act/2010-06/brazil-Turkey-broker-fuel-swap-iran.

Crowcroft, Orlando, "Coronavirus: 'Europe Is in a Fight for Its Life' Says von der Leyen," Euronews, March 26, 2020, https://www.euronews.com/2020/03/26/coronavirus-europe-is-in-a-fight-for-its-life-says-ursula-von-der-leyen.

Cui, Mu, "COVID-19: China Steps in to Help Italy Battle the Virus | DW | 24.03.2020," DW.COM., March 24, 2020, https://www.dw.com/en/covid-19-china-steps-in-to-help-italy-battle-the-virus/a-52901560.

Cumhurbaşkanı Yardımcısı Oktay: Dünyadaki ülkelerin üçte ikisi Türkiye'den yardım talebinde bulundu," Anadolu Agency, May 15, 2020, retrieved June 4, 2020 from https://www.aa.com.tr/tr/koronavirus/cumhurbaskani-yardimcisi-oktay-dunyadaki-ulkelerin-ucte-ikisi-turkiyeden-yardim-talebinde-bulundu/1841441.

Daily Sabah with Anadolu Agency, "NATO Chief Praises Turkey's Efforts for Solidarity amid Coronavirus Pandemic," *Daily Sabah*, April 15, 2020, https://www.dailysabah.com/politics/diplomacy/nato-chief-praises-Turkeys-efforts-for-solidarity-amid-coronavirus-pandemic.

Daily Sabah with Anadolu Agency, "Turkish Aid Agency TIKA Marks 28th Anniversary of Foundation," *Daily Sabah*, January 30, 2020. https://www.dailysabah.com/Turkey/2020/01/30/turkish-aid-agency-tika-marks-28th-anniversary-of-foundation.

Daily Sabah with Anadolu Agency, "Turkey Sends 2nd Batch of Medical Supplies to US amid Coronavirus Pandemic." April 30, 2020, https://www.aa.com.tr/en/americas/turkey-sends-2nd-batch-of-medical-aid-to-virus-hit-us/1823906

Damhuis, Koen, "Why Dutch Populists Are Exceptional," Brookings (blog), November 30, https://www.brookings.edu/articles/why-dutch-populists-are-exceptional/.

Davis, Julie Hirschfeld, "Trump Warns NATO Allies to Spend More on Defense, or Else," *The New York Times*, July 2, 2018, sec. World, https://www.nytimes.com/2018/07/02/world/europe/trump-nato.html.

Dean, Grace, "COVID-19 Vaccines Are Now Being Administered in the UK and US, but the Rollout May Take Years in Poorer Countries. Here Are the Major Challenges They Face," Business Insider, December 20, 2020, https://www.businessinsider.com/poor-countries-may-wait-years-covid-19-vaccines-2020-11.

"Decline of Global Extreme Poverty Continues but Has Slowed," World Bank, September 19, 2018, https://www.worldbank.org/en/news/press-release/2018/09/19/decline-of-global-extreme-poverty-continues-but-has-slowed-world-bank.

Devji, Faisal, "From Xinjiang to Germany: How Did Islamophobia Become a Global Phenomenon?" *The Guardian*, March 27, 2020, http://www.theguardian.com/commentisfree/2020/mar/27/xinjiang-germany-islamophobia-global-phenomenon.

Diamond, Larry, "What Went Wrong in Iraq," *Foreign Affairs* 83 (5): 34–56, 2004, https://doi.org/10.2307/20034066.

"Doctors Expect 'Covid Catastrophe' in Syria," BBC News, October 27, 2020, https://www.bbc.com/news/av/world-middle-east-54697587.

Dodd, Clement, *The History and Politics of the Cyprus Conflict*, Palgrave Macmillan UK, 2010, https://doi.org/10.1057/9780230275287.

"Donald Trump's Immigration Order Is Bad Foreign Policy | National News | US News," US News & World Report, January 30, 2017, //www.usnews.com/news/national-news/articles/2017-01-30/donald-trumps-immigration-order-is-bad-foreign-policy.

Dubosh, Emily, Mixalis Poulakis, and Nour Abdelghani, "Islamophobia and Law Enforcement in a Post 9/11 World," *Islamophobia Studies Journal* 3 (1): 138–57, 2015, https://doi.org/10.13169/islastudj.3.1.0138.

"Dueling U.N. Resolutions on Syria Both Fail, Leaving Millions at Risk," *Washington Post.*, n.d., https://www.washingtonpost.com/national-security/dueling-un-resolutions-on-syria-both-fail-leaving-millions-at-risk/2019/09/19/3d9e71b4-db2d-11e9-a688-303693fb4b0b_story.html.

"Egypt Signs $1 Billion Turkish Loan Deal," Reuters, September 30, 2012, sec. Emerging Markets, https://www.reuters.com/article/us-egypt-Turkey-loan-idUSBRE88T0G920120930.

Einbinder, Nicole, "How the Far Right Has Reshaped the Refugee Debate in Europe," Frontline, January 22, 2018, https://www.pbs.org/wgbh/frontline/article/how-the-far-right-has-reshaped-the-refugee-debate-in-europe/.

Ekman, Mattias, "Anti-Refugee Mobilization in Social Media: The Case of Soldiers of Odin," *Social Media + Society* 4 (1): 2056305118764431. 2018, https://doi.org/10.1177/2056305118764431.

El Menouar, Yasemin and Sasnal Patrycja, "There's a Social Pandemic Poisoning Europe:

Hatred of Muslims | Patrycja Sasnal and Yasemin El Menouar," *The Guardian*, September 28, 2020, http://www.theguardian.com/commentisfree/2020/sep/28/europe-social-pandemic-hatred-muslims-blm.

Elliott, Larry, "The Coronavirus Crisis Has Brought the EU's Failings into Sharp Relief | Larry Elliott," *The Guardian*, March 29, 2020, http://www.theguardian.com/business/2020/mar/29/the-coronavirus-crisis-has-brought-the-eus-failings-into-sharp-relief.

Emami, Gazelle, "24 Is Back to Make You Fear Muslim Terrorists Again," Vulture, n.d., accessed August 10, 2021. https://www.vulture.com/2017/02/24-legacy-muslim-terrorists-terrible-timing.html.

Erdoğan, Recep Tayyip, *A Fairer World Is Possible: A Proposed Model for United Nations Reform*, Turkuvaz Kitap, Istanbul, September 2021.

"Erdoğan Says Turkey Aims to Boost Ties with Libya's GNA," Reuters, October 4, 2020, sec. Emerging Markets, https://www.reuters.com/article/us-libya-security-Turkey-idUSKBN26P0Z3.

Ergocun, Gokhan, "Turkey Remains Most Generous Donor of Humanitarian Aid," Anadolu Agency, September 30, 2019, https://www.aa.com.tr/en/world/Turkey-remains-most-generous-donor-of-humanitarian-aid/1597587.

Erlanger, Steven, "Muslim Countries Denounce French Response to Killing of Teacher, Urge Boycott," *The New York Times*, October 27, 2020, sec. World, https://www.nytimes.com/2020/10/27/world/europe/French-Muslims-Turkey-crackdown.html.

Esen, Hasan, "UK Thanks Turkey for COVID-19 Support," Anadolu Agency, December 4, 2020, https://www.aa.com.tr/en/europe/uk-thanks-Turkey-for-covid-19-support/1801433.

"Europe Experienced a Surge in Government Restrictions on Religious Activity over the Last Decade," Pew Research Center (blog), n.d., https://www.pewresearch.org/fact-tank/2019/07/29/europe-experienced-a-surge-in-government-restrictions-on-religious-activity-over-the-last-decade/.

"Figures at a Glance," UNHCR, June 18, 2020. https://www.unhcr.org/figures-at-a-glance.html.

"Four Things to Know about Covid in the World's Largest Refugee Camp," Oxfam International, March 11, 2021, https://www.oxfam.org/en/blogs/four-things-know-about-covid-worlds-largest-refugee-camp.

Forde, Kaelyn, "DAESH Counting on Anti-Muslim Backlash 'to Sharpen the Divide,' Experts Warn," ABC News, June 7, 2017, https://abcnews.go.com/International/isis-counting-anti-muslim-backlash-sharpen-divide-experts/story?id=47862508.

"France's Election Season Kicks off with Le Pen Sparring on Islam," Bloomberg, February 11, 2021, https://www.bloomberg.com/news/articles/2021-02-11/france-s-election-season-kicks-off-with-le-pen-sparring-on-islam.

Frazee, Gretchen, "What the New Zealand Shootings Tell Us about the Rise in Hate Crimes," PBS NewsHour, March 15, 2019, https://www.pbs.org/newshour/world/what-the-new-zealand-shootings-tell-us-about-the-rise-in-hate-crimes.

"Funding the Fight against COVID-19 in the World's Poorest Countries," United Nations, n.d., https://www.un.org/en/un-coronavirus-communications-team/funding-fight-against-covid-19-world%E2%80%99s-poorest-countries.

Gearan, Anne, "Clinton Seeks to Broaden Ties with Syrian Opposition," *The Washington Post*, August 11, 2012, sec. Middle East. https://www.washingtonpost.com/world/middle_east/clinton-seeks-to-broaden-ties-with-syrian-opposition/2012/08/11/e46e0d4c-e3af-11e1-89f7-76e23a982d06_story.html.

Gilsinan, Kathy, "How China Deceived the WHO," The Atlantic, April 12, 2020, https://www.theatlantic.com/politics/archive/2020/04/world-health-organization-blame-pandemic-coronavirus/609820/.

"Global Humanitarian Assistance Report 2019 - World," ReliefWeb, 2019, https://reliefweb.int/report/world/global-humanitarian-assistance-report-2019.

Goldberg, Jeffrey, "Hillary Clinton: 'Failure' to Help Syrian Rebels Led to the Rise of DAESH," The Atlantic, August 10, 2014, https://www.theatlantic.com/international/archive/2014/08/hillary-clinton-failure-to-help-syrian-rebels-led-to-the-rise-of-isis/375832/.

"Greece: Attacks on Boats Risk Migrant Lives," Human Rights Watch, October 22, 2015, https://www.hrw.org/news/2015/10/22/greece-attacks-boats-risk-migrant-lives.

"Greece: Refugees Attacked and in 'Hellish Conditions' on Kos," Amnesty International, September 4, 2015, https://www.amnesty.org/en/latest/news/2015/09/greece-refugees-attacked-and-in-hellish-conditions-on-kos/.

Gülmez, Seçkin Barış, "The Cyprus Policy of the CHP: Change or Continuation?" *Insight Turkey* 9 (1): 127–38, 2007.

Habib, Mohshin, Christine Jubb, Salahuddin Ahmad, Masudur Rahman, and Henri Pallard, *Forced Migration of Rohingya: The Untold Experience*, Ottawa, Ontario: Ontario International Development Agency, Canada, 2018.

Hall, Richard, "How the Brexit Campaign Used Refugees to Scare Voters," The World from PRX, June 24, 2016, https://www.pri.org/stories/2016-06-24/how-brexit-campaign-used-refugees-scare-voters.

"Harvard-Belfer on Syria: Chemical Weapons," Belfer Center for Science and International Affairs, n.d., https://www.belfercenter.org/harvard-belfer-syria-chemcial-weapons.

Hill, Fiona, "Putin Scores on Syria," Foreign Affairs, September 11, 2013, https://www.foreignaffairs.com/articles/russian-federation/2013-09-11/putin-scores-syria.

"How Egyptians Toppled Mubarak – and Who Will Lead Them Now," *Christian Science Monitor*, February 12, 2011, https://www.csmonitor.com/World/Middle-East/2011/0212/How-Egyptians-toppled-Mubarak-and-who-will-lead-them-now.

"Humanitarian Aid to Syrians Threatened as Russia and China Veto Proposals at U.N," *The Washington Post*, n.d., accessed August 9, 2021, https://www.washingtonpost.com/national-security/humanitarian-aid-to-syrians-threatened-as-russia-and-china-veto-proposals-at-un/2020/07/10/96c87a0c-c2d4-11ea-b178-bb7b05b94af1_story.html.

"IOM Turkey Calls for Greater Assistance for Migrants and Refugees as COVID-19 Restrictions Ease," International Organization for Migration, June 5, 2020, https://www.iom.int/news/iom-Turkey-calls-greater-assistance-migrants-and-refugees-covid-19-restrictions-ease.

"Islamophobia: Understanding Anti-Muslim Sentiment in the West," Gallup.com, December 12, 2011, https://news.gallup.com/poll/157082/islamophobia-understanding-anti-muslim-sentiment-west.aspx.

"Israel: Background and U.S. Relations," EveryCRSReport, n.d., accessed August 9, 2021, https://www.everycrsreport.com/reports/RL33476.html. 58.

Jones, Sophia, "Masked 'Commandos' Are Attacking Refugee Boats off This Idyllic Greek Island," Huffington Post, August 13,.2015, https://www.huffpost.com/entry/greek-migrant-boats-attacked_n_55cbabf1e4b0898c488664e6.

Kanj, Sultan al-, "Humanitarian Disaster Looms over Syria's Idlib amid COVID-19 Surge - Al-Monitor: The Pulse of the Middle East," November 24, 2020, https://www.al-monitor.com/originals/2020/11/syria-idlib-hospitals-surge-coronavirus-cases.html.

Kay, Sean, "What Went Wrong with NATO?" *Cambridge Review of International Affairs* 18 (1): 69–83, 2005, https://doi.org/10.1080/09557570500059589.

Kazanci, Handan, "UN Envoy: Turkey's Refugee Response 'Exemplary,'" Anadolu Agency, November 30, 2019, https://www.aa.com.tr/en/world/un-envoy-Turkeys-refugee-response-exemplary/1659784.

Keohane, Daniel, "The Absent Friend: EU Foreign Policy and Counter-Terrorism," *JCMS: Journal of Common Market Studies* 46 (1): 125-46, 2008, https://doi.org/10.1111/j.1468-5965.2007.00770.x.

Kessler, Glenn, "Analysis | Trump's Outrageous Claim That 'Thousands' of New Jersey Muslims Celebrated the 9/11 Attacks," *The Washington Post*, November 22, 2015, https://www.washingtonpost.com/news/fact-checker/wp/2015/11/22/donald-trumps-outrageous-claim-that-thousands-of-new-jersey-muslims-celebrated-the-911-attacks/.

Khaleeli, Homa, "The Perils of 'Flying While Muslim,'" *The Guardian*, August 8, 2016, http://www.theguardian.com/world/2016/aug/08/the-perils-of-flying-while-muslim.

Kirişci, Kemal, "Turkey's Engagement with Its Neighborhood: A 'Synthetic' and Multidimensional Look at Turkey's Foreign Policy Transformation," *Turkish Studies* 13 (3): 319-41, 2012, https://doi.org/10.1080/14683849.2012.717444.

Kirişci, Kemal and Elizabeth Ferris, "What Turkey's Open-Door Policy Means for Syrian Refugees," *Brookings* (blog), November 30, https://www.brookings.edu/blog/order-from-chaos/2015/07/08/what-Turkeys-open-door-policy-means-for-syrian-refugees/.

Kirkpatrick, David D, "Army Ousts Egypt's President; Morsi Is Taken into Military Custody," *The New York Times*, July 3, 2013, sec. World, https://www.nytimes.com/2013/07/04/world/middleeast/egypt.html.

Kirkpatrick, David D, "Egyptian Presidential Candidate Carries Banner of the Old Order," *The New York Times*, April 8, 2012, sec. World, https://www.nytimes.com/2012/04/09/world/middleeast/omar-suleiman-egypts-new-candidate-represents-old-order.html.

Kishi, Katayoun, "Assaults against Muslims in U.S. Surpass 2001 Level," Pew Research Center (blog), November 15, 2017, https://www.pewresearch.org/fact-tank/2017/11/15/assaults-against-muslims-in-u-s-surpass-2001-level/.

"Kofi Annan's Six-Point Plan," Aljazeera, March 27, 2021, https://www.aljazeera.com/news/2012/3/27/kofi-annans-six-point-plan-for-syria.

Leiby, Richard and Muhammad Mansour, "Arab League Asks U.N. for No-Fly Zone over Libya," *The Washington Post*, March 12, 2011, sec. World, https://

www.washingtonpost.com/world/arab-league-asks-un-for-no-fly-zone-over-libya/2011/03/12/ABoieOR_story.html.

Lenz-Raymann, Kathrin, "Securitization of Islam: A Vicious Circle: Counter-Terrorism and Freedom of Religion in Central Asia" in *Securitization of Islam: A Vicious Circle*, 1–4, Counter-Terrorism and Freedom of Religion in Central Asia, Transcript Verlag, 2014, https://www.jstor.org/stable/j.ctv1fxgjp.1.

Levin, Brian, "Explaining the Rise in Hate Crimes against Muslims in the US," The Conversation, n.d., accessed http://theconversation.com/explaining-the-rise-in-hate-crimes-against-muslims-in-the-us-80304.

Luongo, Michael T, "Traveling While Muslim Complicates Air Travel," *The New York Times*, November 7, 2016, sec. Business, https://www.nytimes.com/2016/11/08/business/traveling-while-muslim-complicates-air-travel.html.

Mahmood, Basit, "Why Muslims Should Still Be Afraid of the Dutch Election Outcome, Even Though Wilders Lost," *The Independent*, March 16, 2017, https://www.independent.co.uk/voices/dutchelectiongeertwildersmarkruttenetherlandspopulismislam-a7632936.html.

Maizland, Lindsay and Eleanor Albert, "What Forces Are Fueling Myanmar's Rohingya Crisis?" Council on Foreign Relations, January 23, 2020, https://www.cfr.org/backgrounder/rohingya-crisis.

Martin, Michel and Arsalan Ifitkhar, "Muslims Are Just the Latest in History of Scapegoats, Author Says," *NPR*, June 5, 2016, sec. Author Interviews, https://www.npr.org/2016/06/05/480861394/muslims-are-just-the-latest-in-history-of-scapegoats-author-says.

Massoumi, Narzanin, "Opinion | Why Is Europe So Islamophobic?" *The New York Times*, March 6, 2020, sec. Opinion, https://www.nytimes.com/2020/03/06/opinion/europe-islamophobia-attacks.html.

McAuley, James, "Macron Outlines New Law to Prevent Islamic 'Separatism' in France," *The Washington Post*, n.d., accessed August 10, 2021, https://www.washingtonpost.com/world/europe/macron-islam-france/2020/10/02/ba8a1dcc-04bc-11eb-b92e-029676f9ebec_story.html.

McKay, Betsy and Drew Hinshaw, "How Coronavirus Overpowered the World Health Organization," *The Wall Street Journal*, August 28, 2020, sec. US, https://www.wsj.com/articles/the-who-was-built-to-guard-global-health-it-was-too-weak-for-coronavirus-11598625537.

Mearsheimer, John J, *The Israel Lobby and U.S. Foreign Policy*, 1st edition, New York: FSG Adult, 2008.

"Migrant Crisis: Migration to Europe Explained in Seven Charts," BBC News, March 4, 2016, sec. Europe, https://www.bbc.com/news/world-europe-34131911.

Misra, Tanvi, "Anti-Muslim Incidents in America, Mapped," Bloomberg, March 9, 2018, https://www.bloomberg.com/news/articles/2018-03-09/anti-muslim-incidents-are-increasing-across-america.

Mohamed, Saira, "Syria, the United Nations, and the Responsibility to Protect," *Proceedings of the Annual Meeting (American Society of International Law)* 106: 223–26, 2012, https://doi.org/10.5305/procannmeetasil.106.0223.

Morelli, Vincent, and Paul Gallis, "NATO in Afghanistan: A Test of the Transatlantic

Alliance," Library of Congress Washington DC Congressional Research Service, 2008, https://apps.dtic.mil/sti/citations/ADA489238.

Moustafa, Tamir, "Drafting Egypt's Constitution: Can a New Legal Framework Revive a Flawed Transition?" SSRN Scholarly Paper ID 2007085, Rochester, NY: Social Science Research Network, 2012, https://doi.org/10.2139/ssrn.2007085.

Mudde, Cas, "Nativism Is Driving the Far-Right Surge in Europe – and It Is Here to Stay," *The Guardian*, November 12, 2019, http://www.theguardian.com/global/commentisfree/2019/nov/12/nativism-is-driving-the-far-right-surge-in-europe-and-it-is-here-to-stay.

Müftüler Baç, Meltem, "Turkey's Political Reforms and the Impact of the European Union," *South European Society and Politics* 10 (1): 17–31, 2005, https://doi.org/10.1080/13608740500037916.

Müller, Marco, "Where Are 'Burqa Bans' in Europe?" Deutsche Welle, January 8, 2019, https://www.dw.com/en/where-are-burqa-bans-in-europe/a-49843292.

Murray, Donette, "The Carcass of Dead Policies: Lessons for Obama in Dealing with Iran," *Contemporary Politics* 16 (2): 209–23, 2010, https://doi.org/10.1080/13569771003783992.

Nadin, Peter, "How the UN Security Council Failed Syria," The Interpreter, August 30, 2017, https://www.lowyinstitute.org/the-interpreter/how-un-security-council-failed-syria.

Namli, Kaan and Fadi Farasin, "Astana: The Rise of a New Alliance and Its Implications for International Relations" in *The Syrian Crisis: Effects on the Regional and International Relations*, edited by Dania Koleilat Khatib, 123–44, Perspectives on Development in the Middle East and North Africa (MENA) Region, Singapore: Springer, 2021, https://doi.org/10.1007/978-981-15-5050-8_8.

"Nato Alliance Experiencing Brain Death, Says Macron," BBC News, November 7, 2019, sec. Europe, https://www.bbc.com/news/world-europe-50335257.

"NATO-UNHCR Airlift Extended as Aid Is Rushed to Pakistan before the Winter," UNHCR, n.d., accessed August 10, 2021. https://www.unhcr.org/news/press/2005/11/436a3cf14/nato-unhcr-airlift-extended-aid-rushed-pakistan-winter.html.

Necat Tasci, Ufuk, "How the UAE, Russia and France Have Teamed up in Libya,' TRT World, 2020, https://www.trtworld.com/magazine/how-the-uae-russia-and-france-have-teamed-up-in-libya-42583.

"New Zealand Mosque Shooting: What Is Known about the Suspect?" BBC News, March 18, 2019, sec. Asia, https://www.bbc.com/news/world-asia-47579243.

"No Need to Give More Right to Speak to Iraqi Pm," Anadolu Agency, April 22, 2012, https://www.aa.com.tr/en/Turkey/no-need-to-give-more-right-to-speak-to-iraqi-pm/372095.

"OHCHR | 37th Session of the Human Rights Council," n.d., accessed August 10, 2021, https://www.ohchr.org/EN/NewsEvents/Pages/DisplayNews.aspx?NewsID=22702&LangID=E.

Osseiran, Nada, and Yemi Lufadeju, "1 in 3 People Globally Do Not Have Access to Safe Drinking Water – UNICEF, WHO," June 18, 2019, https://www.who.int/news/item/18-06-2019-1-in-3-people-globally-do-not-have-access-to-safe-drinking-water-unicef-who.

Parkinson, Joe, "Turkey: Mubarak Should Leave Now," *The Wall Street Journal*,

February 2, 2011, sec. World News, https://www.wsj.com/articles/SB10001424052748703960804576119811353451704.

"Perspective - 'There Is No Evidence That Migrants Steal Jobs,'" France 24, September 2, 2019, https://www.france24.com/en/20190902-perspective-jonathan-portes-economic-impact-migration-migrants-europe-unemployment.

Phillips, Amber, "Donald Trump Calls Profiling Muslims 'Common Sense,'" *The Washington Post,* June 19, 2016, https://www.washingtonpost.com/news/post-politics/wp/2016/06/19/donald-trump-calls-profiling-muslims-common-sense/.

Picheta, Rob, "France's Niqab Ban Violates Human Rights, UN Committee Says," CNN, October 23, 2018, https://www.cnn.com/2018/10/23/europe/france-niqab-ban-un-intl/index.html.

Pickel, Gert and Cemal Öztürk, "The Varying Challenge of Islamophobia for the EU: On Anti-Muslim Resentments and Its Dividend for Right-Wing Populists and Eurosceptics—Central and Eastern Europe in a Comparative Perspective" in *Illiberal Trends and Anti-EU Politics in East Central Europe,* edited by Astrid Lorenz and Lisa H. Anders, 57–80. Palgrave Studies in European Union Politics. Cham: Springer International Publishing, 2020. https://doi.org/10.1007/978-3-030-54674-8_3.

"Pneumonia of Unknown Cause – China," January 5, 2020, https://www.who.int/emergencies/disease-outbreak-news/item/2020-DON229.

"President Erdoğan: Turkey Will Continue Open-Door Policy for Syrian Refugees," *Daily Sabah,* March 13, 2016, https://www.dailysabah.com/politics/2016/03/13/president-Erdoğan-Turkey-will-continue-open-door-policy-for-syrian-refugees.

"Progress on Household Drinking Water, Sanitation and Hygiene 2000-2017," June 14, 2019, https://www.who.int/publications-detail-redirect/9789241516235.

"Poverty and Shared Prosperity 2018," World Bank, n.d., https://www.worldbank.org/en/publication/poverty-and-shared-prosperity-2018.

"Remarks by the President to the White House Press Corps," Whitehouse.Gov., August 20, 2012, https://obamawhitehouse.archives.gov/the-press-office/2012/08/20/remarks-president-white-house-press-corps..

"Report of the WHO-China Joint Mission on Coronavirus Disease 2019 (COVID-19)," n.d., https://www.who.int/publications-detail-redirect/report-of-the-who-china-joint-mission-on-coronavirus-disease-2019-(covid-19).

Rettman, Andrew, "Turkey Calls Emergency Nato Talks on Syria," EUobserver, June 25, 2012, https://euobserver.com/foreign/116743.

Reuters in Berkasovo, "More Than 10,000 Refugees Stranded in Serbia as Borders Close, UNHCR Says," *The Guardian,* October 19, 2015, http://www.theguardian.com/world/2015/oct/19/refugees-stranded-on-serbian-croatian-border.

Richards, Barry, "What Drove Anders Breivik?" *Contexts* 13 (4): 42–47, 2014, https://doi.org/10.1177/1536504214558216.

Roser, Max, Hannah Ritchie, and Bernadeta Dadonaite, "Child and Infant Mortality," *Our World in Data,* May, https://ourworldindata.org/child-mortality.

"Russia and China Veto Draft Security Council Resolution on Syria," UN News, October 4, 2011, https://news.un.org/en/story/2011/10/390412-russia-and-china-veto-draft-security-council-resolution-syria.

"Russia, China Veto Syria Aid via Turkey for Second Time This Week," Reuters, July

10, 2020, sec. China, https://www.reuters.com/article/us-syria-security-un-idUSKBN24B2NW.

Ryan, Missy, and Gillian Brockell, "A War Fought, a War Avoided: Libya and Syria Tested Obama's Core Values," *The Washington Post*, June 3, 2016, https://www.washingtonpost.com/graphics/national/obama-legacy/intervention-libya-and-syrian-crisis.html.

Said, Edward W, *Covering Islam: How the Media and the Experts Determine How We See the Rest of the World*, Revised edition, New York: Vintage, 1997.

Sarsar, Saliba, "The Question of Palestine and United States Behavior at the United Nations," *International Journal of Politics, Culture, and Society* 17 (3): 457-70, 2004, https://doi.org/10.1023/B:IJPS.0000019613.01593.5e.

Scahill, Jeremy and Murtaza Hussain, "The Changing of the Overlords: From the Rubble of the U.S. War in Iraq, Iran Built a New Order," *The Intercept* (blog), November 18, 2019, https://theintercept.com/2019/11/18/us-iraq-invasion-iran/.

"Security Concerns of Muslim Communities," n.d., https://www.osce.org/odihr/infographic-muslim-security-guide.

"Security Council Backsliding on Duty to Protect Syria's Civilians, Rights Advocate Stresses, amid Calls to Protect Hospitals, Review Deconfliction Accords | Meetings Coverage and Press Releases," n.d., accessed August 10, 2021, https://www.un.org/press/en/2019/sc13903.doc.htm.

"Security Council Imposes Additional Sanctions on Iran, Voting 12 in Favour to 2 Against, with 1 Abstention | Meetings Coverage and Press Releases," UN Security Council, June 9, 2010, https://www.un.org/press/en/2010/sc9948.doc.htm.

"Security Council Unanimously Adopts Resolution 2254 (2015), Endorsing Road Map for Peace Process in Syria, Setting Timetable for Talks | Meetings Coverage and Press Releases," n.d., https://www.un.org/press/en/2015/sc12171.doc.htm.

Shadid, Anthony, "Resurgent Turkey Flexes Its Muscles Around Iraq," *The New York Times*, January 5, 2011, sec. World, https://www.nytimes.com/2011/01/05/world/middleeast/05turkey.html.

"Shocking Images of Drowned Syrian Boy Show Tragic Plight of Refugees," *The Guardian*, September 2, 2015. http://www.theguardian.com/world/2015/sep/02/shocking-image-of-drowned-syrian-boy-shows-tragic-plight-of-refugees.

Sissons, Miranda and Abdulrazzaq Al-Saeidi, "Iraq's de-Baathification Still Haunts the Country," Aljazeera, n.d., https://www.aljazeera.com/opinions/2013/3/12/iraqs-de-baathification-still-haunts-the-country.

Slovic, Paul, Daniel Västfjäll, Arvid Erlandsson, and Robin Gregory, "Iconic Photographs and the Ebb and Flow of Empathic Response to Humanitarian Disasters," *Proceedings of the National Academy of Sciences* 114 (4): 640-44, 2017, https://doi.org/10.1073/pnas.1613977114.

Sözen, Ahmet and Kudret Özersay, "The Annan Plan: State Succession or Continuity," *Middle Eastern Studies* 43 (1): 125–41, 2007, https://doi.org/10.1080/00263200601079773.

Stack, Liam, "In Slap at Syria, Turkey Shelters Anti-Assad Fighters," *The New York Times*, October 27, 2011, sec. World, https://www.nytimes.com/2011/10/28/world/europe/Turkey-is-sheltering-antigovernment-syrian-militia.html.

"Statistics," n.d., https://www.mpac.org/programs/hate-crime-prevention/statistics.php.

Strakes, Jason E., "Current Political Complexities of the Iraqi Turkmen," *Iran & the Caucasus* 13 (2): 365–82, 2009, https://www.jstor.org/stable/25703815.

Strømmen, Hannah, "Christian Terror in Europe? The Bible in Anders Behring Breivik's Manifesto," *Journal of the Bible and Its Reception* 4 (1): 147–69, 2017, https://doi.org/10.1515/jbr-2017-2006.

"Syria Chemical Attack: What We Know," BBC News, September 24, 2013, sec. Middle East, https://www.bbc.com/news/world-middle-east-23927399.

"Syria," 2021, Global Centre for the Responsibility to Protect, May 31, 2021, https://www.globalr2p.org/countries/syria/.

"Syria: Seven Years of Catastrophic Failure by the International Community," March 15, 2018, https://www.amnesty.org/en/latest/news/2018/03/syria-seven-years-of-catastrophic-failure-by-the-international-community/.

"Syrian Arab Republic: Recent Developments in Northwestern Syria Situation Report No. 24 - As of 26 January 2021 - Syrian Arab Republic," ReliefWeb, n.d., https://reliefweb.int/report/syrian-arab-republic/syrian-arab-republic-recent-developments-northwestern-syria-situation-14.

Tardy, Thierry, "COVID-19: Shaping Future Threats and Security Policies," COVID-19: NATO Defense College, 2020, https://www.jstor.org/stable/resrep25148.8.

Thakur, Ramesh, "Libya and the Responsibility to Protect: Between Opportunistic Humanitarianism and Value-Free Pragmatism," *Security Challenges* 7 (4): 13–25, 2011.

Thakur, Ramesh, "R2P after Libya and Syria: Engaging Emerging Powers," *The Washington Quarterly* 36 (2): 61–76, 2013, https://doi.org/10.1080/0163660X.2013.791082.

"'Their Goal Is to Destroy Everyone': Uighur Camp Detainees Allege Systematic Rape," BBC News, February 2, 2021, sec. China, https://www.bbc.com/news/world-asia-china-55794071.

"The Eastern Mediterranean Tinderbox: Why Greek-Turkish Rivalries Have Expanded," BBC News, August 25, 2020, sec. Europe, https://www.bbc.com/news/world-europe-53906360.

"TİKA Continues to Be Lifeblood with Water Wells Drilled in Afghanistan - TİKA." n.d., accessed August 9, 2021, https://www.tika.gov.tr/en/news/tika_continues_to_be_lifeblood_with_water_wells_drilled_in_Afghanistan-19192.

"Timeline of the Muslim Ban," ACLU of Washington, May 23, 2017, https://www.aclu-wa.org/pages/timeline-muslim-ban.

"Timeline: WHO's COVID-19 Response," n.d., https://www.who.int/emergencies/diseases/novel-coronavirus-2019/interactive-timeline.

Tisdall, Simon, "Turkey Calls on Major Powers to Intervene in Syria," *The Guardian*, October 19, 2012, http://www.theguardian.com/world/2012/oct/19/Turkey-britain-us-intervene-syria.

Tocci, Nathalie, "Reflections on Post-referendum Cyprus," *The International Spectator* 39 (3): 39–50, 2004, https://doi.org/10.1080/03932720408457082.

"Toward Long-Term Solidarity with Syrian Refugees? Turkey's Policy Response and Challenges," *Atlantic Council* (blog), September 20, 2018, https://www.atlanticcouncil.org/in-depth-research-reports/report/toward-long-term-solidarity-with-syrian-refugees-Turkey-s-policy-response-and-challenges/.

Trilling, Daniel, "'Protecting the European Way of Life' from Migrants Is a Gift to the Far Right," *The Guardian*, September 13, 2019, http://www.theguardian.com/commentisfree/2019/sep/13/protecting-europe-migrants-far-right-eu-nationalism.

Tufekci, Zeynep, "The WHO Shouldn't Be a Plaything for Great Powers," The Atlantic, April 16, 2020, https://www.theatlantic.com/health/archive/2020/04/why-world-health-organization-failed/610063/.

"Turkey Offers to Resume Israel-Syria Mediation," Reuters, January 29, 2010, sec. World News, https://www.reuters.com/article/us-Turkey-israel-idUSTRE60S59420100129.

"Turkey Opposes Any NATO Operation in Libya," Reuters, March 14, 2011, sec. Editor's Picks,https://www.reuters.com/article/us-libya-Turkey-idUSTRE72D49D20110314.

"Turkey Rejects U.S. Troop Proposal", CNN, March 2, 2003, "https://www.cnn.com/2003/WORLD/meast/03/01/sprj.irq.main/.

"Turkey Reluctantly Joins NATO Operations against Libya," France 24, March 24, 2011, https://www.france24.com/en/20110324-Turkey-allows-nato-command-libya-military-operations-vote.

"Turkey Tells Mubarak to Listen to the People," Reuters, February 1, 2011, sec. Editor's Picks,https://www.reuters.com/article/us-egypt-Turkey-idUSTRE71047Y20110201.

"Turkey's PM Erdoğan Urges Col Muammar Gaddafi to Quit," BBC News, May 3, 2011, sec. Europe, https://www.bbc.com/news/world-europe-13265825.

"Turkish Development Assistance Reports - TİKA," 2019, https://www.tika.gov.tr/en/publication/list/turkish_development_assistance_reports-24.

"Turkish PM Calls on Syria's Assad to Quit," Reuters, November 22, 2011, sec. World News, https://www.reuters.com/article/us-Turkey-syria-idUSTRE7AL0WJ20111122.

"Turkish President Erdoğan Remarks at United Nations General Assembly - General Debate | C-SPAN.Org," September 19, 2017, https://www.c-span.org/video/?434273-6/turkish-president-erdoan-remarks-united-nations-general-assembly-general-debate.

"Turkish Red Crescent Provides Tents for Idlib Refugees - Turkey News," *Hürriyet Daily News*, n.d., accessed August 9, 2021, https://www.hurriyetdailynews.com/turkish-red-crescent-provides-tents-for-idlib-refugees-152105.

"Turkey | Global Focus," December 20, 2019, https://reporting.unhcr.org/Turkey.

"Turkey Keeps Breaking Records in Humanitarian Aid and Development Assistance - TİKA," n.d., https://www.tika.gov.tr/en/news/Turkey keeps_breaking_records_in_humanitarian_aid_and_development_assistance-49351.

"Turkey Provides Medical Aid to 53 Countries to Tackle Coronavirus Pandemic," *Daily Sabah*, April 24, 2020, https://www.dailysabah.com/politics/Turkey-provides-medical-aid-to-53-countries-to-tackle-coronavirus-pandemic/news.

"Turkey: Sustainable Development Knowledge Platform," n.d., accessed August 9, 2021. https://sustainabledevelopment.un.org/memberstates/Turkey.

"Türkiye'den Yemen'de İç Savaş Mağdurlarına Gıda Yardımı," TİKA - Türk Birliği ve Koordinasyon Ajansı Başkanlığı, n.d. www.tika.gov.tr/tr/haber/turkiye_den_yemen'de_ic_savas_magdurlarina_gida_yardimi-57696.

Türk, Volker, and Madeline Garlick, "From Burdens and Responsibilities to Opportunities: The Comprehensive Refugee Response Framework and a Global Compact on Refugees," *International Journal of Refugee Law* 28 (4): 656-78, 2016. https://doi.org/10.1093/ijrl/eew043.

"UN General Assembly Urges Greater Protection for Palestinians, Deplores Israel's 'Excessive' Use of Force," UN News, June 13, 2018, https://news.un.org/en/story/2018/06/1012162.

"UN Security Council 'Utterly Failed' Syrian Detainees; A Victim Voices Her Plea to 'End Impunity and Stop This Horror,'" UN News, August 7, 2019, https://news.un.org/en/story/2019/08/1043891.

Usher, Graham, "Letter from the UN: After the U.S. Veto on Settlements," *Journal of Palestine Studies* 40 (3): 74–83, 2011, https://doi.org/10.1525/jps.2011.xl.3.74.

Ustun, Kadir and Nuh Yilmaz, "The Erdoğan Effect: Turkey, Egypt and the Future of the Middle East," *The Cairo Review of Global Affairs*, October 17, 2011, https://www.thecairoreview.com/essays/the-Erdoğan-effect-Turkey-egypt-and-the-future-of-the-middle-east/.

Üstün, Kadir, "Turkey Iran Policy: Between Diplomacy and Sanctions," *Insight Turkey* 12 (3): 19–26, 2010, https://www.jstor.org/stable/26334100

Virchow, Fabian, "PEGIDA: Understanding the Emergence and Essence of Nativist Protest in Dresden," *Journal of Intercultural Studies* 37 (6): 541–55, 2016, https://doi.org/10.1080/07256868.2016.1235026.

Wahab, Bilal, "Iraq and KRG Energy Policies: Actors, Challenges and Opportunities," Foreign Policy Initiative, n.d., https://policycommons.net/artifacts/1478837/iraq-and-krg-energy-policies/2137779/.

Walker, Peter, "Syria and Israel Officially Confirm Peace Talks," *The Guardian*, May 21, 2008, http://www.theguardian.com/world/2008/may/21/israelandthepalestinians.syria.

Welsh, Jennifer M, "The Responsibility to Protect after Libya & Syria," *Daedalus* 145 (4): 75–87, 2016, https://doi.org/10.1162/DAED_a_00413.

Western, Jon, and Joshua S. Goldstein, "R2P After Syria," Foreign Affairs, November 27, 2013, https://www.foreignaffairs.com/articles/syria/2013-03-26/r2p-after-syria.

Wildman, Sarah, "Meet the Far-Right Party That's Bringing Racism and Xenophobia Back to Germany," Vox, September 26, 2017, https://www.vox.com/world/2017/9/26/16360916/afd-german-far-right-racism-xenophobia.

Wilkes, Sybella, "Syria Crisis: UNHCR Urges European Union States to Honour Their Asylum System Principles," UNHCR, n.d., accessed August 10, 2021. https://www.unhcr.org/news/latest/2012/10/507d4c586/syria-crisis-unhcr-urges-european-union-states-honour-asylum-system-principles.html.

Wilson, Chris, and Sanjal Shastri, "Hate Crimes against Muslims Spiked after the Mosque Attacks, and Ardern Promises to Make Such Abuse Illegal," The Conversation, n.d., http://theconversation.com/hate-crimes-against-muslims-spiked-after-the-mosque-attacks-and-ardern-promises-to-make-such-abuse-illegal-147347.

Wilson, Scott, and Joby Warrick, "Assad Must Go, Obama Says," *The Washington Post*, August 18, 2011, sec. Politics, https://www.washingtonpost.com/politics/assad-must-go-obama-says/2011/08/18/gIQAelheOJ_story.html

Wood, Daniel, "As Pandemic Deaths Add Up, Racial Disparities Persist — And in Some Cases Worsen," *NPR*, September 23, 2020, sec. Coronavirus By The Numbers, https://www.npr.org/sections/health-shots/2020/09/23/914427907/as-pandemic-deaths-add-up-racial-disparities-persist-and-in-some-cases-worsen.

"World's Most Vulnerable Countries Lack the Capacity to Respond to a Global Pandemic Credit: MFD/Elyas Alwazir | Office of the High Representative for the Least Developed Countries, Landlocked Developing Countries and Small Island Developing States," n.d., https://www.un.org/ohrlls/news/world%E2%80%99s-most-vulnerable-countries-lack-capacity-respond-global-pandemic-credit-mfdelyas-alwazir.

World Health Organization (WHO), "Preliminary Investigations Conducted by the Chinese Authorities Have Found No Clear Evidence of Human-to-Human Transmission of the Novel #coronavirus (2019-NCoV) Identified in #Wuhan, #China. Https://T.Co/Fnl5P877VG," Twitter, January 14, 2020, https://twitter.com/WHO/status/1217043229427761152.

Yarar, Eralp, "Despair Replaces Hope, Risk of Coronavirus Outbreak Threatens Idlib," *Daily Sabah*, April 9, 2020, https://www.dailysabah.com/politics/news-analysis/despair-replaces-hope-risk-of-coronavirus-outbreak-threatens-idlib.

"Yemen Refugee Crisis: Aid, Statistics and News | USA for UNHCR," n.d., https://www.unrefugees.org/emergencies/yemen/.

Zenko, Micah, "What Obama Really Meant by 'No Boots on the Ground,'" The Atlantic, December 3, 2015, https://www.theatlantic.com/international/archive/2015/12/obama-boots-on-the-ground/418635/.

"204,000 Syrian Refugees Returned to Idlib since March, Turkey Records," *Daily Sabah*, July 19, 2020, https://www.dailysabah.com/politics/204000-syrian-refugees-returned-to-idlib-since-march-Turkey-records/news.

INDEX

K

L

M

N

O

P

R

S